Physical Characteristics of the English Foxhound

(from the American Kennel Club breed standard)

Back and Loin: Must both be very muscular, running into each other without any contraction between them. The couples must be wide, even to raggedness, and the topline of the back should be absolutely level.

Stern: Well set on and carried gaily but not in any case curved over the back like a squirrel's tail. The end should taper to a point and there should be a fringe of hair below.

Hindquarters: Required to be very strong, and as endurance is of even greater consequence than speed, straight stifles are preferred.

Legs: As straight as a post, and as strong; size of bone at the ankle being especially regarded as all important.

Color and Coat: Not regarded as very important, so long as the former is a good "hound color," and the latter is short, dense, hard, and glossy. Hound colors are black, tan, and white, or any combination of these three, also the various "pies" compounded of white and the color of the hare and badger, or yellow, or tan.

Feet: In all cases should be round and catlike, with well-developed knuckles and strong horn, which last is of the greatest importance.

D1264817

English Foxhound

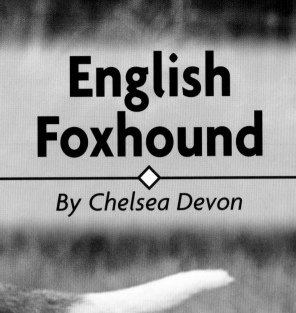

By Chelsea Devon

9
History of the English Foxhound

A regal hound with a long-standing association with the British fox hunt, the English Foxhound derived from various hound types. Trace the breed's development, including obstacles along the way and revitalization of type. Meet important Masters of Foxhounds who were instrumental in shaping the breed we know today.

19
Characteristics of the English Foxhound

A hunting breed with strong pack instincts, the English Foxhound can present challenges and rewards to the pet owner. Find out what the breed requires to flourish in a pet home to determine if you are a suitable Foxhound owner. The pros and cons are discussed, as well as how to find the dog for you and potential health concerns in the breed.

31
Breed Standard for the English Foxhound

Learn the requirements of a well-bred English Foxhound by studying the description of the breed set forth in the American Kennel Club standard. Both show dogs and pets must possess key characteristics as outlined in the breed standard.

39
Your Puppy English Foxhound

Be advised about choosing a reputable breeder and selecting a healthy, typical puppy. Understand the responsibilities of ownership, including home preparation, acclimatization, the vet and prevention of common puppy problems.

58
Everyday Care of Your English Foxhound

Enter into a sensible discussion of dietary and feeding considerations, exercise, grooming, traveling and identification of your dog. This chapter discusses English Foxhound care for all stages of development.

74
Training Your English Foxhound

By Charlotte Schwartz
Be informed about the importance of training your English Foxhound from the basics of housebreaking and understanding the development of a young dog to executing obedience commands (sit, stay, down, etc.).

Contents

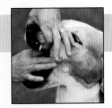

KENNEL CLUB BOOKS: **ENGLISH FOXHOUND**
ISBN: 1-59378-352-3

Copyright © 2004
Kennel Club Books, Inc., 308 Main Street, Allenhurst, NJ 07711 USA
Cover Design Patented: US 6,435,559 B2 • Printed in South Korea

Photography by Michael Trafford, with additional photos by
Norvia Behling, T.J. Calhoun, Carolina Biological Supply, Doskocil, Isabelle Francais, James Hayden-Yoav, James R. Hayden, RBP, Carol Ann Johnson, Bill Jonas, Dwight R. Kuhn, Dr. Dennis Kunkel, Mikki Pet Products, Phototake, Jean Claude Revy, Dr. Andrew Spielman and Alice van Kempen.

Illustrations by Patricia Peters.

The publisher would like to thank all of the owners of the dogs featured in this book, including Mrs. Janet Nolan and Giselle Soskar.

The English Foxhound today is still known primarily for the breed's intended function and skills as a hunting dog. Foxhounds are more frequently seen in hunting packs or competing in organized hunting events than in show rings and pet homes.

HISTORY OF THE
ENGLISH FOXHOUND

The English Foxhound derived from lines of expertly bred, skilled hunting dogs that have inhabited the French country-side for hundreds of years. Over this time period, these talented hunting breeds, which may have originally developed from other hunting-dog variations, slowly transformed into the breed that we know and respect today—the English Foxhound. Variations of the breed were frequently portrayed in writings, works of famous painters and creations of early well-respected talented sketchers and sculptors. Even today, the breed is regularly displayed in such works.

The English Foxhound was first admired for its extraordinary hunting skills. It wasn't long before the human race recognized and utilized the breed's ability to track and bring down large game. English Foxhounds were extremely quick, athletic and built for stamina, which enabled them to hunt for long hours, even days, with minimal rest and care.

Originally, the English Foxhound was used to assist

Francisco José de Goya painted "Charles III, as a Huntsman" in 1786. The king is pictured with his hunting companion, a dog that resembles an all-white Foxhound.

Foxhounds descended from various other types of hound, including the French hunting dogs known as Gascon Hounds. The largest of the Gascon varieties, the Grande Bleu de Gascogne, is shown here.

farmers in the control of fox, which often ate their chickens, lambs and other valuable farm animals. However, eventually, over time, the fox became less and less of a threat to farm life. This is when fox hunting turned into more of a sport rather than a way of life. Theoretically, it was no longer fox hunting, but more like fox "chasing." Fox hunting as a sport involved the pursuit of red and gray foxes, bobcats and coyotes.

ENGLISH HERITAGE
As a direct result of French importation, English Foxhounds are descendants of many early hound varieties. Although it is not known for sure (and probably will never be 100% confirmed), there is some solid proof that the breed derived from the Gascon Hounds. Gascon Hounds were quite similar to today's Bloodhound and once populated south-western France. There is also some speculation that the

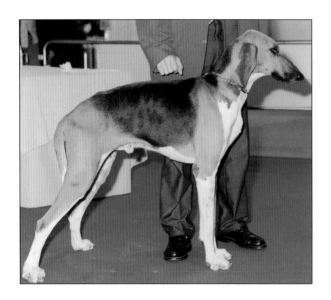

Another of the French hunting hounds is the Poitevin. The breed was used successfully for hunting wolves. The French Revolution and an 1842 rabies outbreak decimated the breed, leaving only one dog and two bitches. All present-day Poitevins developed from those three specimens.

English Foxhound has a direct link to the Southern Hound or St. Hubert Hound. This large hound had an excellent nose and loud bark.

Still another breed that existed during this early period was the Northern Hound. The Northern Hound had many Greyhound-like characteristics. It was much more slender, lighter boned and speedier than the Southern Hound, but lacked the nose and cry of its nearby southern cousin. It only made sense that the Northern and Southern varieties would someday be crossed. Each hound type had its own positive qualities, which could only benefit one another if mixed, and later would aid in the hunter's pursuit of large game.

The two hounds merged and were later considered "staghounds."

It wasn't until the early 17th century that the English Foxhound lived up to its name and was used primarily as a fox-hunter. Early variations of the breed chased and hunted larger game, such as deer. By the early 1700s, because the breed was considered too slow and too bulky, breeders attempted to produce a lighter and leaner dog. Most early attempts to do so were unsuccessful until the early 1800s.

In 1819, a dog by the name of Belvoir Furrier emerged. He was considered to be the best-bred hound of his time. He was bred at Belvoir, and quickly distinguished himself as a top hunter and producer in the field. His hunting ability was unmatched by his peers.

The first hound show in Great Britain took place in 1859. The event was led by Thomas Parrington and was held on the

TRACING TYPES

In the early 1900s, the Masters of Foxhounds Association was developed. This organization is important for tracking and tracing many different English Hound pedigrees. Two types of English Foxhounds existed: the "old" English variety and the "modern" English type.

The Gascon Hound varieties, from left to right: the Petit Bleu de Gascogne, Basset Bleu de Gascogne, Griffon Bleu de Gascogne and Grand Bleu de Gascogne.

This depiction of Foxhounds by the renowned canine artist Reinagle first appeared in *The Sportsmen's Cabinet* in 1803; it later was published in the early 1900s with the title "Typical Foxhounds of 100 Years Ago."

grounds at Redcar. The show included classes for "single unentered hounds" (those that did not hunt yet), "single entered hounds" (those that did hunt) and "couples." After the Redcar shows, Peterborough became the main area for most of the early pre-20th century hound events.

By the beginning of the 20th century, many English Foxhounds began to lose their qualities of voice and nose. This was unacceptable for a breed meant to be a reliable hunter. In addition, many were losing their stamina in the field and began showing signs of poor structure and conformation. For those

hounds that knuckled over, the term "shorthorn" was established and widely used.

Recognizing the urgency to do something to save the breed, dedicated breeders and hunters made strong efforts to revive the English Foxhound and restore

The Foxhound "Wildair" was a winner in the 1930s. He is pictured here winning at the Cambridgeshire show in the UK.

Masters of Hounds from English descent became active breeders exclusively for the English Stud Book. These individuals included Duke of Rutland of the Belvoir, Lord Yarborough of the Brocklesby and Lord Daresbury of the Limerick. The packs that these individuals developed were considered pure English. While these Masters of Hounds were concerned with establishing pure English packs, the Welsh Hounds of the French were more interested in outcrossing to pursue better scenting hounds with better voice. A strong voice was important so the hound could be heard at great distances in the field, and a good nose was essential because the hunters could not always follow directly behind the pack.

the breed back to its earlier status as a dependable, durable hunting companion. Two top hounds of this era that established themselves as good examples of the breed were dogs named Wiseacre and Waverly. Wiseacre won Best Single Unentered Dog Hound at England's Peterborough show of 1911, and Waverly took the title of Champion Dog Hound at the same show. A few years later in 1924, South Staffordshire Denmark won the Dog Hound Championship at Peterborough. These three dogs became the backbone of the early 20th-century development of the English Foxhound.

In efforts to further develop the breeding program of the English Foxhound, three

In 1925, Sir Edward was the first to cross the rough-coated

THE FOXHOUND'S ABILITIES

The English Foxhound should possess a good nose and voice, and be fully capable of moving through fields over the length of a day's hunt. In recent years, the breed is used mainly on fox hunts, but is equally capable of tracking down larger game.

hound with the Peterborough-type hound. This new and improved hound became eligible for the English Stud Book in 1955.

THE ENGLISH FOXHOUND IN NORTH AMERICA

The English Foxhound has always been well known on American soil. The first known Master of Hounds to settle in North America was Robert Brooke of Maryland in 1650. In 1691, Mike Dixon convinced the court system that his pack of cherished hounds, which were said to be pestering innocent bystanders, were actually able hunting companions used to hunt and kill wild fox, wolves and other large game animals. It was at this time in history that several hundred English Foxhounds were imported to America. The breed's demand quickly increased after its skills as an avid hunter became better recognized.

In 1738, Lord Fairfax imported several top hunting dogs to the United States. Fairfax is said to have hunted with George Washington, who had his own prized collection of hounds.

Despite the breed's gradual increase in popularity in the US, it took more than 100 years before the Foxhound Stud Book of America was formed in 1890.

However, nearly 125 years before this Stud Book registry came to be, the Gloucester Foxhunting Club of Philadelphia was established. In October of 1766, the club sponsored the first organized hunt. The club fell apart by 1818. The Montreal Hunt in Canada, founded in 1826, was the earliest established hunt that is still actively functioning today in North America.

Some other early fox-hunting organizations that have had a lasting impact on the progress and advancement of the breed include the Piedmont Foxhounds (established in 1840) and the Rose Tree Fox Hunting

"The Death of the Fox," from an engraving by P.C. Canot, was based on the 1770 painting by J. Wootton.

"Foxhounds," a painting by J. Emms of dogs owned by Walter Hutchinson. To the right of the Foxhounds is a game terrier, whose job it was to turn out the fox when it went to earth.

Club of 1853. The Piedmont Foxhounds were established in Virginia and are still in existence today. The Rose Tree Fox Hunting Club came into existence when two individuals by the names of Mr. J. Howard Lewis and Mr. George E. Darling decided that they were too old to ride horseback and started a walking stake instead.

Although there were many 19th-century American dogs that paved the way for the breed, one dog by the name of Tuck and another by the name of Trailer won first prize as Best Couple in 1879 at the Delaware Agricultural and Industrial Society.

The first Foxhound field trial in the US took place in 1889. Prior to 1909, there was no distinction between English and American Foxhounds. The trial was won by a dog named Joe Forrester, owned by Dr. A. C. Heffinger. In addition to hound shows, it wasn't long before the English Foxhound could also enter regular all-breed shows. In 1909, the first English Foxhound was registered with the American Kennel Club. The dog's name was "Auditor AKC 129533" and he was owned by Clarence Moore of Washington, DC and Mrs. O. Pryce-Rice of Lianwrda, South Wales. Most of the early hounds were English imports. The first American show champion of record was Langley Drag AKC 132378, owned by Major W. A. Phipps from Los Angeles.

Although the breed's popularity in the show ring has remained minimal, many excellent representatives of the breed have emerged over the years. Ch. Mr. Stewart's Cheshire Winslow remains one of the top dogs on record. This multiple Best-in-Show dog had

PRESIDENT AND HUNTER
George Washington was an avid fox-hunter and owned several of his own dogs. Although little documentation is available from this time period, reliable diaries recovered from early settlers reveal Washington's fondness for the breed.

several group wins, including a Group One at the prestigious Westminster Kennel Club Show in 1983. Although English Foxhound AKC registration numbers are small, a good percentage of these dogs earn their champion titles.

The Fife Foxhound Pack at a meet in the early 1900s.

Then and now: (Top) A meet at Stretton, circa 1853, features hunters in top hats and an assemblage of about 40 English Foxhounds. Fox-hunting is a pastime deeply rooted in Britain. (bottom) While traditional hunts still take place, the Foxhound today is also seen in hound shows and competitive hunting events. These modern-day events preserve customary dress and procedures.

CHARACTERISTICS OF THE
ENGLISH FOXHOUND

IS THE ENGLISH FOXHOUND RIGHT FOR YOU?

Choosing a new puppy is the beginning of a long-term commitment. A dog is something that you are likely to have for the next decade (or more), something that you want to make 100% sure you're going to be happy with and something that needs to match your lifestyle, limitations and expectations. It's safe to say that not all breeds are good for everyone. It's imperative that you choose a dog that will flourish in the environment in which you are planning to keep him, and one that has characteristics that appeal to you. Otherwise, it can make for an unhappy situation for both the dog and the owner. It's vital that you do your research before rushing out and purchasing a dog of any breed.

The English Foxhound is not found very often as a household pet, and is favored more for its hunting skills and abilities afield. However, the English Foxhound can and will make an excellent home companion, provided you understand the breed's particular needs and requirements.

The English Foxhound is a very distinguished and unique breed. It's a superlative hunter with an excellent nose, impressive voice, great speed and exceptional endurance. It has a large head, a long nose, low-set ears, long and muscular shoulders and a deep chest. The coat is short, dense and shiny, and usually seen in tan, black, white or a combination of the three. The breed's coat requires minimal grooming with the exception of weekly once-overs with a brush and an occasional bath. The breed is an average shedder.

The English Foxhound is more heavily built than its American cousin. English Foxhounds are hot-trailing hounds, which usually require more direction from their huntsman than do the American strains. A majority of English Foxhound owners keep them in packs rather than by themselves, but this is not to say that they can't be housed separately. If you are looking for a pet, it may be best to obtain your puppy from a

WOOLLIES
The rough-coated variety of the English Foxhound that evolved from the Duke of Beaufort's hound pack was sometimes referred to as "woollies."

A pack dog by nature, a Foxhound greatly enjoys the company of other dogs.

show line rather than an established field line.

Due to their history as pack kennel hounds, they don't always easily adjust to house-pet environments. However, English Foxhounds will adjust to normal household settings provided they are allowed adequate exercise. These dogs need to run! They have extremely high energy levels. Keeping them isolated in an apartment setting won't do the trick. They make poor city dogs. An English Foxhound requires daily exposure to a large fenced yard or fenced-in field where he can run freely. If he does not get the required exercise, he can become restless and destructive. An English Foxhound can exercise on a large farm or in a large yard for several hours and still be enthusiastic and eager for more!

Keep in mind that the English Foxhound has been bred as a pack-hunting dog. Attempting to change these natural instincts is a losing battle in most cases. These dogs have been bred to run long distances under adverse weather conditions, while working their best when within a pack setting. Potential owners must keep this in mind before deciding to keep an English Foxhound as a pet, as the breed needs its special requirements met in order to do well in an ordinary household.

English Foxhounds are extremely intelligent dogs, but can be poor participants in obedience. They can be stubborn in their ways, which can make them sometimes difficult to train. Diligence and patience in training are the keys to success in any endeavor, from basic commands to preparing for competition. You'll always have to stay one step ahead of your English Foxhound.

While the English Foxhound was not bred to be a family pet, if

THE HUNTING HOUND
The goal of most English Foxhound breeders is to produce a pack of hounds that will run quickly, give great tongue (known as a cry), show stamina and have keen noses. Each hound receives his commands from the huntsman based on the body position of the huntsman and his horse.

your dog is well socialized as a young puppy, he will adapt to family life. This is a lively, friendly, happy-go-lucky breed of dog. English Foxhounds love children and will bond easily with family members. The breed has a tendency to roam, and thus should always be on-lead or in secure areas. It will usually adapt quickly to a new environment if properly cared for. English Foxhounds are exceptionally athletic and very eager to work. They are very willing and eager to please their owners and family members. However, this can sometimes be on the breed's own terms! All of these considerations need to be borne in mind before deciding that the English Foxhound is the breed for you.

One thing that's certain is that the Foxhound needs exercise and plenty of it. The ideal Foxhound owner will have a large, securely enclosed area in which his dog can run and play to his heart's content.

FINDING THE ENGLISH FOXHOUND THAT'S RIGHT FOR YOU

If you are sure that you can provide the right environment and care for an English Foxhound, and

that the relationship will be a mutually happy one, you should then begin your search for a puppy. The key to finding a healthy and sound English Foxhound begins by contacting reputable breeders. The American Kennel Club and national Foxhound breed clubs (such as the English Foxhound Club of America, Masters of Foxhounds Association of America and Foxhound Club of North America)

SIZE DIFFERENCES

The English Foxhound resembles the American Foxhound, differing mainly in size and build, with the English type being a bit taller and larger. The English Foxhound stands 23–27 inches tall and weighs 55–75 pounds. The American Foxhound stands 22–25 inches high and weighs about 50–65 pounds. The American breed also has a narrower chest.

can refer you to prospective breeders in your region. Another good way to meet breeders and make contacts within the breed is to visit a dog show or hunting event. Be prepared to do some research and traveling. Since the English Foxhound is not one of the more popular breeds, you may have to drive several hours away to find a breeder, depending on where you live.

Once you find a breeder with whom you feel comfortable, make arrangements to visit his kennel. The puppies and adult dogs that you meet there must be friendly and outgoing. If the puppy's sire and dam are on the premise (at least one of them should be), kindly ask to see them so that you can evaluate their appearance and temperament. Are they healthy and sound, both physically and temperamentally?

In making your selection, you should respect the opinions and suggestions of the breeder. Make it very clear as to what type of dog you are looking for. Are you planning to hunt with your new puppy? Are you looking for a potential show dog? Are you looking for solely a family companion? Are you interested in a male or female? How about a young dog or an older one? Be prepared to answer questions about your own dog-caring experience. Many responsible breeders are very selective about the

Despite the fact that the Foxhound is first and foremost a hunting dog, his loyalty to and bond with his owner when kept as a pet are something that can't be denied.

individuals to whom they sell their dogs. Reputable breeders are understandably concerned as to where the dogs from their kennel will be going and whether the dogs will be cared for and housed properly.

THE SPORT OF FOX-HUNTING
Fox-hunting has existed in England and America for several hundred years. The sport of fox-hunting involves mounted riders' chasing wild quarry over large expanses of land. The rules of the hunt can vary from country to country; in the US, the hunt ends when the fox is accounted for by entering a hole in the ground. It's truly a miraculous sight to observe and hear a group of hounds and men working as a courageous team. While the sport was once considered something in which only the wealthy participated, that assumption has since changed in recent decades. Now, many different groups are currently involved with the sport. There are close to 200 sanctioned hunts held each year.

Fox-hunting is a highly systematized sport. The generic term "fox-hunting" applies to red fox, gray fox, coyote and bobcat. The type of animal hunted depends on the geographic location. The Masters of Foxhounds Association of America heads all fox-hunting events. This is a non-profit organi-

zation that was formed to maintain high sporting standards, approve and register hunting territories and register eligible Foxhounds (this includes English, American and crossbred Foxhounds, and Harriers). The organization insists on compliance with its rules and does its best to supervise the conduct of its sport. Typically, an individual pays a modest fee to be a member of a hunt. The excitement and thrill of the chase are what attracts many people to this fascinating sport. Part of the excitement is that it's never clear as to what path a wild fox may take.

An individual designated as the "master" is responsible for the day's hunt and makes all the decisions regarding that hunt. The master is also responsible for supervising breeding programs and appointing a hunt staff to work with them. If the master doesn't lead the hunt himself, he appoints a "fieldmaster." It's the fieldmaster's job to keep the field of riders close to the pack, but not so close as to interfere with the huntsman hunting his dogs. Individuals called "whippers-in" assist the huntsman in hunting the hounds. They are used to help prevent hounds from running onto roads or land not open to hunting. There is a formal dress code for all fox-hunters, which usually includes black leather boots, a tie, breeches and a protec-

The always-on-the-go Foxhound is a naturally hardy breed, and breeders strive to produce hounds that are sound, athletic and capable of great endurance.

tive hat. Members who are a part of the field workers wear black or red coats, although exact attire and colors vary depending on the country in which the hunt is taking place.

If the excitement of galloping over beautiful countryside on an athletic horse isn't breathtaking enough, the sight of a pack of hounds working together in full cry is truly incredible. People of all ages and social backgrounds enjoy this wonderful sport.

BREED-SPECIFIC HEALTH CONCERNS

Prospective owners should be aware of the health issues that can occur in the breed. To be fore-warned is to be forearmed, so

acquainting yourself with these potential problems will help you be more prepared if you decide to own an English Foxhound.

Fortunately, the English Foxhound is a very healthy breed. Since this hound has been bred for hunting under adverse conditions (rough terrain and climate), a general toughness has been instituted within the breed, which has allowed it to avoid many of the ailments that commonly affect other dogs. The breed is free of many genetic disorders that plague other large breeds. However, there are a few potential health concerns of which all owners and breeders should be aware.

It's highly recommended that

all new dog owners check with their breeders in regard to potential health risks that may exist within individual bloodlines. Reputable breeders should be honest when it comes to something as important as the health and well-being of their puppies. Following are some of the more common ailments that you may encounter as a new English Foxhound owner.

HIP DYSPLASIA

Canine hip dysplasia is a congenital defect that is a common source of lameness in many medium- to large-sized dogs. The early signs of hip dysplasia are usually recognizable. If a dog appears lame or has some difficulty when attempting to sit or lie down, he may be suffering from hip dysplasia. The beginning symptoms may be difficult to diagnose at first, because they are usually slow to develop. However, dogs that suffer from the disease usually develop arthritis in the hip joint because of the abnormal strain placed on the joints themselves. Although it is not critical, it's recommended that English Foxhound owners have their dogs x-rayed to check for the condition. Breeders, of course, should have their stock x-rayed and cleared of the condition before the dogs are incorporated into breeding programs.

Research has found that restricting some environmental stress can protect genetically pre-dysplastic dogs. There is even some indication that some dog foods that are currently on the market for puppies might help the condition manifest, meaning that foods that promote rapid growth can put undue strain on a pup's developing joints and limbs. Allowing for a more stable and uniform growth may be your best protective measure.

ENTROPION

Entropion is usually a congenital defect that involves the abnormal condition in which the eyelid rolls in toward the eye. Frequently, this condition causes the lashes to rub against the cornea and causes much irritation. Surgical correction is required to correct the problem.

ECTROPION

The opposite of entropion is ectropion, in which the lower eyelid rolls away from the eyeball. The condition is usually hereditary, but can be caused by injury. Surgery can restore the eyelids to their proper location.

BLOAT

Bloat (gastric dilatation/torsion) is a serious condition that affects many breeds of dog. If a dog does not receive immediate medical aid when the condition occurs, he can easily die. Large, deep-chested dogs such as the English Foxhound are

DO YOU KNOW ABOUT HIP DYSPLASIA?

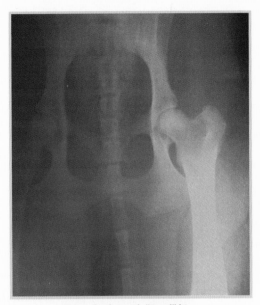

X-ray of a dog with "Good" hips.

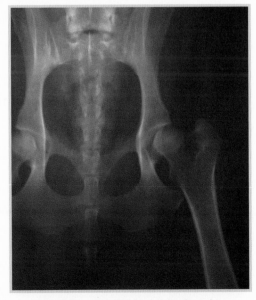

X-ray of a dog with "Moderate" dysplastic hips.

Hip dysplasia is a fairly common condition found in pure-bred dogs. When a dog has hip dysplasia, his hind leg has an incorrectly formed hip joint. By constant use of the hip joint, it becomes more and more loose, wears abnormally and may become arthritic.

Hip dysplasia can only be confirmed with an x-ray, but certain symptoms may indicate a problem. Your dog may have a hip dysplasia problem if he walks in a peculiar manner, hops instead of smoothly runs, uses his hind legs in unison (to keep the pressure off the weak joint), has trouble getting up from a prone position or always sits with both legs together on one side of his body.

As the dog matures, he may adapt well to life with a bad hip, but in a few years the arthritis develops and many dogs with hip dysplasia become crippled.

Hip dysplasia is considered an inherited disease and only can be diagnosed definitively by x-ray when the dog is two years old, although symptoms often appear earlier. Some experts claim that a special diet might help your puppy outgrow the bad hip, but the usual treatments are surgical. The removal of the pectineus muscle, the removal of the round part of the femur, reconstructing the pelvis and replacing the hip with an artificial one are all surgical interventions that are expensive, but they are usually very successful. Follow the advice of your veterinarian.

Foxhound owners must pay attention to the health of their dog's skin and coat, as a dog that spends much time outdoors can encounter many insects, allergens and other irritants.

frequently affected. An affected dog's stomach fills with gas or fluids and, as a result, swells and twists. The end result is death unless immediate veterinary treatment is administered. Even then, there is no guarantee that a dog that is suffering from the condition will recover.

Some causes of bloat include the dog's eating a large meal, drinking large quantities of water and exercising too soon before or after eating (exercise should be restricted for at least an hour before and two to three hours after meals).

HYPOTHYROIDISM

A dog suffering from hypothyroidism usually loses hair on his flanks and back. In more serious cases, scaling and seborrhea are possible. Inadequate hormone levels are the cause of the condition. Fortunately, although many breeds suffer from hypothyroidism, the condition is easily treated with medication prescribed by the veterinarian.

ANATOMY OF THE EYE

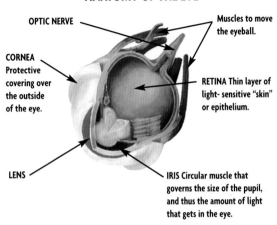

OPTIC NERVE

Muscles to move the eyeball.

CORNEA Protective covering over the outside of the eye.

RETINA Thin layer of light-sensitive "skin" or epithelium.

LENS

IRIS Circular muscle that governs the size of the pupil, and thus the amount of light that gets in the eye.

PROGRESSIVE RETINAL ATROPHY

More familiarly known as PRA, this is a degenerative disease of the retinal visual cells, which eventually progresses to the point of blindness. It is a genetic disease that affects many types of dogs. Dogs that are affected will show early signs of the disease. At first, they have difficulties seeing at night or in dim light. Eventually, the disease can lead to total blindness.

A CLOSER LOOK AT THE RETINA

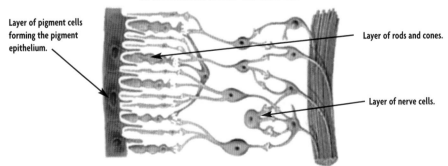

Layer of pigment cells forming the pigment epithelium.

Layer of rods and cones.

Layer of nerve cells.

English Foxhound head study in profile.

A well-constructed English Foxhound.

ENGLISH FOXHOUND

WHY IS THE STANDARD IMPORTANT?

Every breed that's recognized by the American Kennel Club has an official written description known as the breed standard. The standard is written up and presented by the breed's parent club. An official standard represents what the ideal physical description, or "blueprint," of the breed should be. However, the standard is not the representation of any actual dog; rather, it simply is an educated theory of what the ideal representative of the breed should look like. A breed standard is used as a measuring stick for judging conformation dog shows and a goal for which breeders strive with every mating.

At a dog show, a conformation judge evaluates each entrant. It is the judge's duty to choose the specimen in each class that he believes to most closely resemble the breed standard. Not only are proper physical appearance and conformation important but sound temperament and correct movement also are essential for any pure-bred dog.

It's not uncommon for judges to disagree about which dogs are best, and placements can change from day to day or week to week. The standard leaves a lot of room for personal interpretation. This is what makes dog show competition so appealing to both the

MEETING THE IDEAL

The American Kennel Club defines a standard as: "A description of the ideal dog of each recognized breed, to serve as an ideal against which dogs are judged at shows." This "blueprint" is drawn up by the breed's recognized parent club, approved by a majority of its membership and then submitted to the AKC for approval. This is a complete departure from the way standards are handled in the English Foxhound's homeland, where all standards and changes are controlled by England's Kennel Club.

The AKC states that "An understanding of any breed must begin with its standard. This applies to all dogs, not just those intended for showing." The picture that the standard draws of the dog's type, gait, temperament and structure should be the guiding image used by breeders as they plan their programs.

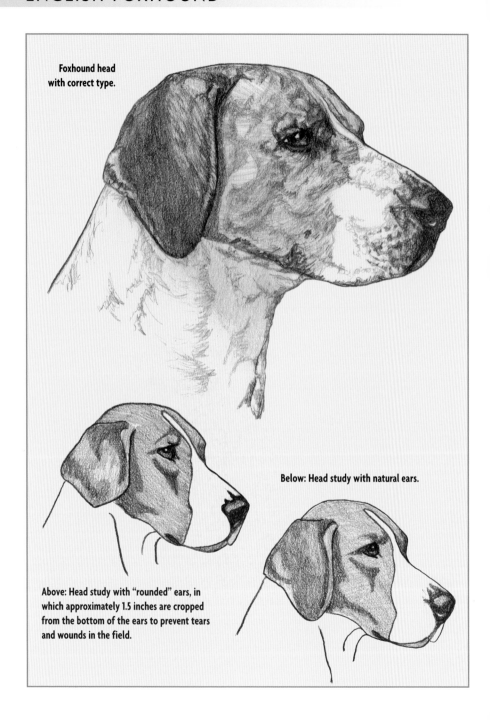

Foxhound head with correct type.

Above: Head study with "rounded" ears, in which approximately 1.5 inches are cropped from the bottom of the ears to prevent tears and wounds in the field.

Below: Head study with natural ears.

professional and novice. Each show circuit brings a completely different judging panel and usually different opinions as to which entrants most closely adhere to the standard. If your dog is an excellent example of the breed, odds are that more than a handful of judges will respect and reward the dog's favorable features.

HOW CAN THE STANDARD HELP YOU?

Understanding the breed standard can be a valuable asset for both the novice and experienced dog owner, and is essential for the handler, breeder and conformation judge. Any person interested in purchasing a dog should thoroughly study the breed standard. It is a valuable guideline in determining the physical qualities that make up your breed of choice, as well as some of the disqualifications that you should be aware of before buying, breeding or judging a member of the breed.

Although the ideal dog represented in the breed standard will probably never exist in actuality, it is in the best interest of all dog fanciers to learn what the standard calls for and for breeders to breed as close to the ideal as possible. It can only help in perpetuating the desired characteristics of the breed and ensure that the breed stays true to type from one generation to the next.

THE AMERICAN KENNEL CLUB STANDARD FOR THE FOXHOUND (ENGLISH)

Head: Should be of full size, but by no means heavy. Brow pronounced, but not high or sharp. There should be a good length and breadth, sufficient to give in a dog hound a girth in front of the ears of fully 16 inches. The nose should be long (4.5 inches) and wide, with open nostrils. Ears set on low and lying close to the cheeks. Most English hounds are "rounded" which means that about 1.5 inches is taken off the end of the ear. The teeth must meet squarely, either a pig-mouth (overshot) or undershot being a disqualification.

Neck: Must be long and clean, without the slightest throatiness, not less than 10 inches from cranium to shoulder. It should taper nicely from shoulders to head, and the upper outline should be slightly convex.

The **Shoulders** should be long and well clothed with muscle, without being heavy, especially at the points. They must be well sloped, and the true arm between the front and the elbow must be long and muscular, but free from fat or lumber. ***Chest and Back Ribs—*** The chest should girth over 31 inches in a 24-inch hound, and the back ribs must be very deep.

Back and Loin: Must both be very muscular, running into each other without any contraction between them. The couples must be wide, even to raggedness, and the topline of the back should be absolutely level, the **Stern** well set on and carried gaily but not in any case curved over the back like a squirrel's tail. The end should taper to a point and there should be a fringe of hair below. The **Hindquarters** or propellers are required to be very strong, and as endurance is of even greater consequence than speed, straight stifles are preferred to those much bent as in a Greyhound. **Elbows** set quite straight, and neither turned in nor out are a *sine qua non.* They must be well let down by means of the long true arm above mentioned.

Legs and Feet: Every Master of Foxhounds insists on legs as straight as a post, and as strong; size of bone at the ankle being

English Foxhound dog in profile, showing correct type, structure, balance and proportion.

FAULTS IN PROFILE

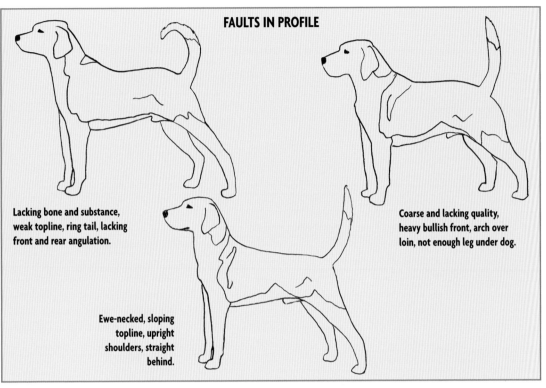

Lacking bone and substance, weak topline, ring tail, lacking front and rear angulation.

Coarse and lacking quality, heavy bullish front, arch over loin, not enough leg under dog.

Ewe-necked, sloping topline, upright shoulders, straight behind.

COMPARISON OF AMERICAN AND ENGLISH FOXHOUND

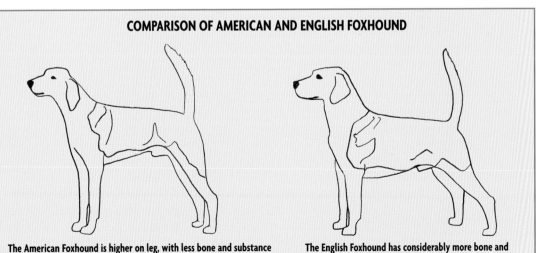

The American Foxhound is higher on leg, with less bone and substance and less angulation front and rear, with an arch over the loin.

The English Foxhound has considerably more bone and substance, built closer to the ground.

Color and Coat: Not regarded as very important, so long as the former is a good "hound color," and the latter is short, dense, hard, and glossy. Hound colors are black, tan, and white, or any combination of these three, also the various "pies" compounded of white and the color of the hare and badger, or yellow, or tan. The *Symmetry* of the Foxhound is of the greatest importance, and what is known as "quality" is highly regarded by all good judges.

Scale of Points

Head	5
Neck	10
Shoulders	10
Chest and back ribs	10
Back and loin	15
Hindquarters	10
Elbows	5
Legs and feet	20
Color and coat	5
Stern	5
Symmetry	5
TOTAL	**100**

Disqualification: Pig-mouth (overshot) or undershot.

The hindquarters are the Foxhound's "propellers" and must be strong and sound for speed and, more importantly, endurance.

especially regarded as all important. The desire for straightness had a tendency to produce knuckling-over, which at one time was countenanced, but in recent years this defect has been eradicated by careful breeding and intelligent adjudication, and one sees very little of this trouble in the best modern Foxhounds. The bone cannot be too large, and the feet in all cases should be round and catlike, with well-developed knuckles and strong horn, which last is of the greatest importance.

The feet, shown from two angles, showing proper rounded shape and development.

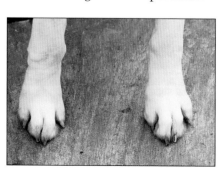

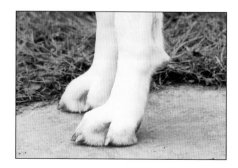

The standard refers to requirements set forth by Masters of Foxhounds, alluding to the fact that all of the breed's desired structural and character traits are intended to produce a dog that is first and foremost a hunter.

The Foxhound's intelligence is evident even at a young age. Don't be fooled by these youngsters' serious expressions, though—they are as curious, playful and mischievous as any pup!

ENGLISH FOXHOUND

COMMITMENT OF OWNERSHIP

We've already discussed the personality and requirements of the breed to help you decide if the English Foxhound is the right dog for you. We've also discussed how to go about finding a breeder and selecting your puppy. After considering all of these factors, you have most likely already made some very important decisions. If you have chosen the English Foxhound as your breed of choice, you have decided which characteristics you want in a dog and what type of dog will best fit into your family and lifestyle.

If you have selected a breeder, you have gone a step further—you have done your research and found a responsible, conscientious person who breeds quality English Foxhounds and who should be a reliable source of help as you and your puppy adjust to life together. If you have observed a litter in action, you have obtained a firsthand look at the dynamics of a puppy "pack" and, thus, you should have learned about each pup's individual personality—perhaps you have even found one that particularly appeals to you.

TEMPERAMENT COUNTS

Your selection of a good puppy can be determined by your needs. A hunting dog, a show potential or a good pet? It is your choice. Every puppy, however, should be of good temperament. Although there are some differences between field and show lines, all responsible breeders strive for good temperament. Do not buy from a breeder who concentrates solely on physical aspects at the expense of personality.

However, even if you have not yet found the English Foxhound puppy of your dreams, observing pups will help you learn to recognize certain behavior and to determine what a pup's behavior indicates about his temperament. You will be able to pick out which pups are the leaders, which ones are less outgoing, which ones are confident, which ones are shy, playful, friendly, aggressive, etc. Equally as important, you will learn to recognize what a

Breeders provide early socialization by playing and spending time with the pups. This dog-human interaction is necessary for easing the pups' transition from canine to human pack.

PUPPY APPEARANCE
Your puppy should have a well-fed appearance but not a distended abdomen, which may indicate worms or incorrect feeding, or both. The body should be firm, with a solid feel. The skin of the abdomen should be pale pink and clean, without signs of scratching or rash. Check the legs to see if the dewclaws have been removed, as this is done at just a few days old.

healthy pup should look and act like. All of these things will help you in your search, and when you find the English Foxhound that was meant for you, you will know it!

Researching your breed, selecting a responsible breeder and observing as many pups as possible are all important steps on the way to dog ownership. It may seem like a lot of effort…and you have not even brought the pup home yet! Remember, though, you cannot be too careful when it comes to deciding on the type of dog you want and finding out about your prospective pup's background. Buying a puppy is not—or *should not* be—just a whimsical purchase. This is one instance in which you actually do get to choose your own family! You may be thinking that buying a puppy should be fun—it should not be so serious and so much work. Keep in mind that your puppy is not a cuddly stuffed toy or decorative lawn ornament, but a creature that will become a real member of your family. You will come to realize that, while buying a puppy is a pleasurable and exciting endeavor, it is not something to be taken lightly. Relax...the fun will start when the pup comes home!

Always keep in mind that a puppy is nothing more than a baby in a furry disguise...a baby

ARE YOU PREPARED?

Unfortunately, when a puppy is bought by someone who does not take into consideration the time and attention that dog ownership requires, it is the puppy who suffers when he is either abandoned or placed in a shelter by a frustrated owner. So all of the "homework" you do in preparation for your pup's arrival will benefit you both. The more informed you are, the more you will know what to expect and the better equipped you will be to handle the ups and downs of raising a puppy. Hopefully, everyone in the household is willing to do his part in raising and caring for the pup. The anticipation of owning a dog often brings a lot of promises from excited family members: "I will walk him every day," "I will feed him," "I will house-train him," etc., but these things take time and effort, and promises can easily be forgotten once the novelty of the new pet has worn off.

who is virtually helpless in a human world and who trusts his owner for fulfillment of his basic needs for survival. In addition to food, water and shelter, your pup needs care, protection, guidance and love. If you are not prepared to commit to these things, then you are not prepared to own a dog.

"Wait a minute," you say. "How hard could this be? All of my neighbors own dogs and they seem to be doing just fine. Why should I have to worry about all of this?" Well, you should not worry about it; in fact, you will probably find that once your English

Observe the puppy with at least one of the parents. They should interact well together and the parent should be sound, both physically and temperamentally, giving you an idea of how your pup will mature.

PEDIGREE VS. REGISTRATION CERTIFICATE

Too often new owners are confused between these two important documents. Your puppy's pedigree, essentially a family tree, is a written record of a dog's genealogy of three generations or more. The pedigree will show you the names as well as performance titles of all dogs in your pup's background. Your breeder must provide you with a registration application, with his part properly filled out. You must complete the application and send it to the AKC with the proper fee. Every puppy must come from a litter that has been AKC-registered by the breeder, born in the USA and from a sire and dam that are also registered with the AKC.

The seller must provide you with complete records to identify the puppy. The AKC requires that the seller provide the buyer with the following: breed; sex, color and markings; date of birth; litter number (when available); names and registration numbers of the parents; breeder's name; and date sold or delivered.

difficult to raise a curious and exuberant English Foxhound pup to be a well-adjusted and well-mannered adult dog—a dog that could be your most loyal friend.

PREPARING PUPPY'S PLACE IN YOUR HOME

Researching your breed and finding a breeder are only two aspects of the "homework" you will have to do before bringing your English Foxhound puppy home. You will also have to prepare your home and family for the new addition. Much like you would prepare a nursery for a newborn baby, you will need to designate a place in your home that will be the puppy's own. How you prepare your home will depend on how much freedom the dog will be allowed. Will he be confined to a specific area in the house, or will he be allowed to roam as he pleases? How much time will he spend indoors versus outdoors? Whatever you decide, you must ensure that he has a place that he can call his own.

When you bring your new puppy into your home, you are bringing him into what will become his home as well. Obviously, you did not buy a puppy so that he could take charge and "rule the roost" in your home, but in order for a puppy to grow into a stable, well-adjusted dog, he has to feel comfortable in his surroundings.

Foxhound pup gets used to his new home, he will fall into his place in the family quite naturally. But it never hurts to emphasize the commitment of dog ownership. With some time and patience, it is really not too

Remember, he is leaving the warmth and security of his mother and littermates, as well as the familiarity of the only place he has ever known, so it is important to make his transition as easy as possible. By preparing a place in your home for the puppy, you are making him feel as welcome as possible in a strange new place. It should not take him long to get used to it, but the sudden shock of being transplanted is somewhat traumatic for a young pup. Imagine how a small child would feel in the same situation—that is how your puppy must be feeling. It is up to you to reassure him and to let him know, "Little fellow, you are going to like it here!"

WHAT YOU SHOULD BUY

CRATE

To someone unfamiliar with the use of crates in dog training, it

Many breeders use large pens or crates to house their litters, which means that the pups should have little trouble adjusting to crates in their new homes if introduced to them right away.

may seem like punishment to shut a dog in a crate, but this is not the case at all. More and more breeders and trainers worldwide are recommending crate-training as the preferred training method for show and pet dogs alike.

Crates are not cruel—crates have many humane and highly effective uses in dog care and training. For example, crate training is a very popular and very successful housebreaking method, a crate can keep your dog safe during travel and, perhaps most importantly, a crate provides your dog with a place of his own in your home. It serves as a "doggie bedroom" of sorts—your English Foxhound can curl up in his crate when he wants to sleep or when he just needs a break.

BOY OR GIRL?

An important consideration to be discussed is the sex of your puppy. For a family companion, a bitch may be the better choice, considering the female's inbred concern for all young creatures and her accompanying tolerance and patience. It is always advisable to spay a pet bitch or neuter a pet male, which may guarantee your Foxhound a longer life.

Your local pet shop should have a large array of crates from which you are sure to find one suitable for your Foxhound. Get one large enough for a full-grown dog.

PHOTO COURTESY OF DOSKOCIL

Many dogs sleep in their crates overnight. When lined with soft bedding and with his favorite toy inside, a crate becomes a cozy pseudo-den for your dog. Like his ancestors, he too will seek out the comfort and retreat of a den—you just happen to be providing him with something a little more luxurious than what his early ancestors enjoyed.

As far as purchasing a crate, the type that you buy is up to you. It will most likely be one of the two most popular types: wire or fiberglass. There are advantages and disadvantages to each type. For example, a wire crate is more open, allowing the air to flow through and affording the dog a view of what is going on around him, while a fiberglass crate is sturdier. Both types can double as car-travel crates, providing protection for the dog when you're on the road.

The size of the crate is another thing to consider. Puppies do not stay puppies forever—in fact, sometimes it seems as if they grow right before your eyes. A small crate may be fine for a very young English Foxhound pup, but it will not do him much good for long! Unless you have the money and the inclination to buy a new crate every time your pup has a growth spurt, it is better to get one from the outset that will accommodate your dog both as a pup and at full size. Keep in mind your English Foxhound's eventual height of around 25 inches at the shoulder, and purchase a large crate that will allow him ample room to stand up, lie down and stretch out.

BEDDING
A soft lambswool crate pad and perhaps a blanket or two in the dog's crate will help him feel more at home. First, the bedding will take the place of the leaves, twigs, etc., that the pup would use in the wild to make a den; the pup can make his own "burrow"

in the crate. Although your pup is far removed from his den-making ancestors, the denning instinct is still a part of his genetic makeup. Second, until you bring your pup home, he has been sleeping amid the warmth of his mother and littermates, and while a blanket is not the same as a warm, breathing body, it still provides heat and something with which to snuggle. You will want to wash your pup's bedding frequently in case he has a potty accident in his crate, and replace or remove any blanket or padding that becomes ragged and starts to fall apart.

Toys

Toys are a must for dogs of all ages, especially for curious, playful pups. Puppies are the "children" of the dog world, and what child does not love toys? Chew toys provide enjoyment to both dog and owner—your dog will enjoy playing with his favorite toys, while you will enjoy the fact that they distract him from your expensive shoes and leather sofa. Puppies love to chew; in fact, chewing is a physical need for pups as they are teething, and everything looks appetizing! The full range of your possessions—from old dish rag to Oriental rug—are fair game in the eyes of a teething pup. Puppies are not all that discerning when it comes to finding something to literally "sink their teeth into"—

TOYS, TOYS, TOYS!

With a big variety of dog toys available, and so many that look like they would be a lot of fun for a dog, be careful in your selection. It is amazing what a set of puppy teeth can do to an innocent-looking toy, so, obviously, safety is a major consideration. Be sure to choose the most durable products that you can find. Hard nylon bones and toys are a safe bet, and many of them are offered in different scents and flavors that will be sure to capture your dog's attention. It is always fun to play a game of fetch with your dog, and there are balls and flying discs that are specially made to withstand dog teeth.

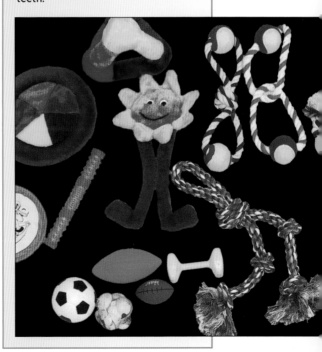

A lightweight yet sturdy nylon lead will be fine for your Foxhound pup. As your dog grows bigger and stronger, you will need an accordingly stronger lead.

everything tastes great!

Only the strongest, most durable toys should be offered to your English Foxhound pup. Hard rubber or nylon bones are popular and safe chew devices, as are strong knotted rope toys. Many of these come in different flavors to attract the dog's attention. Breeders advise owners to resist stuffed toys, because they can become de-stuffed in no time. The overly excited pup may ingest the stuffing, which is neither nutritious nor digestible.

Similarly, squeaky toys are quite popular, but must be avoided for free play. Perhaps a squeaky toy can be used as an aid in training, but not when the pup is unsupervised. If a pup

"disembowels" one of these, the small plastic squeaker inside can be dangerous if swallowed. Monitor the condition of all your pup's toys carefully and get rid of any that have been chewed to the point of becoming potentially dangerous.

Be careful of natural bones, which have a tendency to splinter into sharp, dangerous pieces. Also be careful of rawhide, which can turn into pieces that are easy to swallow or into a mushy mess on your carpet.

LEAD

A nylon lead is probably the best option, as it is the most resistant to puppy teeth should your pup take a liking to chewing on his lead. Of course, this is a habit that should be nipped in the bud, but, if your pup likes to chew on his lead, he has a very slim chance of being able to chew through the strong nylon. Nylon leads are also lightweight, which is good for a young English Foxhound who is just getting used to the idea of walking on a lead. For everyday walking and safety purposes, the nylon lead is a good choice.

As your pup grows up, and becomes larger and stronger, you will need to upgrade his lead accordingly. The lead may be the most important accessory for your English Foxhound, as his strong chase and scenting instincts will have him off and running in a

CHOOSE AN APPROPRIATE COLLAR

The **BUCKLE COLLAR** is the standard collar used for everyday purposes. Be sure that you adjust the buckle on growing puppies. Check it every day. It can become too tight overnight! These collars can be made of leather or nylon. Attach your dog's identification tags to this collar.

The **CHOKE COLLAR** is designed for training. It is constructed of highly polished steel so that it slides easily through the stainless steel loop. The idea is that the dog controls the pressure around his neck and he will stop pulling if the collar becomes uncomfortable. It should be used *only* during training and *never* left on a dog.

The **HALTER** is for a trained dog that has to be restrained to prevent running away, chasing a cat and the like. Considered the most humane of all collars, it is frequently used on smaller dogs on which collars are not comfortable.

Choose durable bowls that can be cleaned easily. Some bowls come mounted on their own stands, or you can purchase stands on which to elevate your dog's bowls separately. This should be considered mandatory to protect your dog from bloat.

PHOTO COURTESY OF MIKKI PET PRODUCTS.

second if not on lead. Thus, your Foxhound should only be let off-lead in securely enclosed areas.

COLLAR

Your pup should get used to wearing a collar all the time since you will want to attach his ID tags to it. Plus, you have to attach the lead to something! A lightweight nylon buckle collar is a good choice, as this type of collar is adjustable and can be increased in size as the pup grows. Make sure that it fits snugly enough so that the pup cannot wriggle out of it, but is loose enough so that it will not be uncomfortably tight around the pup's neck. Check it every day; puppies grow quickly and the collar can become too tight almost overnight! You should be able to fit a finger between the pup and the collar.

It may take some time for your pup to get used to wearing the collar, but soon he will not even notice that it is there. Choke and check collars are made for training, but should only be used by owners who know how to use them properly.

FOOD AND WATER BOWLS

Your pup will need two bowls, one for food and one for water. You may want two sets of bowls, one for inside and one for outside, depending on where the dog will be fed and where he will be spending most of his time.

Stainless steel or sturdy plastic bowls are popular choices. Plastic bowls are more chewable, but dogs tend not to chew on the steel variety, which can be sterilized. It is important to buy sturdy bowls since anything is in danger of being chewed by puppy teeth. You do not want your dog to be constantly chewing apart his bowl (for his safety and your wallet!).

As a preventative measure against the potentially fatal bloat, you should consider it mandatory to purchase stands on which to elevate your English Foxhound's bowls. Bowl stands will usually be available at your pet-supply store. Elevating your dog's food and water aids his digestion and prevents him from having to bend down to reach his bowls, which prevents him from swallowing air, a major cause of bloat.

Cleaning Supplies

Until your pup is house-trained, you will be doing a lot of cleaning. "Accidents" will occur, which is okay in the beginning because the puppy does not know any better. All you can do is be prepared to clean up any accidents. Old rags, towels, newspapers and a safe disinfectant are good to have on hand.

Beyond the Basics

The items previously discussed are the bare necessities. You will find out what else you need as

you go along—grooming supplies, flea/tick protection, baby gates to partition a room, etc. These things will vary depending on your

NATURAL TOXINS

Examine your grass and landscaping before bringing your dog home. Many varieties of plants have leaves, stems or flowers that are toxic if ingested, and you can depend on a curious dog to investigate them. Ask your vet for information on poisonous plants or research them at your library.

If you see your dog carrying a piece of vegetation in his mouth, approach him in a quiet, disinterested manner, avoid eye contact, pet him and gradually remove the plant from his mouth. Alternatively, offer him a treat and maybe he'll drop the plant on his own accord. Be sure no toxic plants are growing in your own yard or kept in your home.

situation, but it is important that right away you have everything you need to feed and make your English Foxhound comfortable in his first few days at home.

PUPPY-PROOFING YOUR HOME
Aside from making sure that your English Foxhound will be comfortable in your home, you also have to make sure that your home is safe for your English Foxhound. This means taking precautions that your pup will not get into anything he should not get into and that there is nothing

within his reach that may harm him should he sniff it, chew it, inspect it, etc. This probably seems obvious since, while you are primarily concerned with your pup's safety, at the same time you do not want your belongings to be ruined. Breakables should be placed out of reach if your dog is to have full run of the house. If he is to be limited to certain places within the house, keep any potentially dangerous items in the "off-limits" areas.

An electrical cord can pose a danger should the puppy decide to taste it—and who is going to convince a pup that it would not make a great chew toy? Cords should be fastened tightly against the wall, out of puppy's sight and reach. If your dog is going to spend time in a crate, make sure that there is nothing near his crate that he can reach if he sticks his curious little nose or paws through the openings. Just as you would with a child, keep all household cleaners and chemicals where the pup cannot get to them; antifreeze is especially dangerous to dogs.

It is also important to make sure that the outside of your home is safe. Of course, your puppy should never be unsupervised, but a pup let loose in the yard will want to run and explore, and he should be granted that freedom. Do not let a fence give you a false sense of security; you would be

Any Foxhound puppy can plead or melodiously howl the old refrain, "Don't fence me in!"

surprised how crafty (and persistent) a dog can be in figuring out how to dig under and squeeze his way through small holes, or to jump or climb over a fence. The English Foxhound was born to run and is very athletic, and loves to follow his nose, so keep this in mind when trying to keep him safely confined. Make the fence high enough so that it really is impossible for your dog to get over it (about 6 feet should suffice), and well embedded into the ground. Be sure to secure any gaps in the fence. Check the fence periodically to ensure that it is in good shape and make repairs as needed; a very determined pup may return to the same spot to "work on it" until he is able to get through.

FIRST TRIP TO THE VET
You have picked out your puppy, and your home and family are ready. Now all you have to do is collect your English Foxhound from the breeder and the fun begins, right? Well…not so fast. Something else you need to prepare is your pup's first trip to the veterinarian. Perhaps the breeder can recommend someone in the area who specializes in hounds or working dogs, or maybe you know some other dog owners who can suggest a good vet. Either way, you should have an appointment arranged for your pup before you pick him up and plan on taking him for an

HOW VACCINES WORK
If you've just bought a puppy, you surely know the importance of having your pup vaccinated, but do you understand how vaccines work? Vaccines contain the same bacteria or viruses that cause the disease you want to prevent, but they have been chemically modified so that they don't cause any harm. Instead, the vaccine causes your dog to produce antibodies that fight the harmful bacteria. Thus, if your dog is exposed to the disease in the future, the antibodies will destroy the viruses or bacteria. Adult dogs are protected by booster shots as needed throughout their lives.

examination before bringing him home or very soon thereafter.

The pup's first visit will consist of an overall examination to make sure that he does not have any problems that are not apparent to you. The veterinarian will also set up a schedule for the pup's vaccinations; the breeder will inform you of which ones the pup has already received and the vet can continue from there.

CRATE-TRAINING TIPS

During crate training, you should partition off the section of the crate in which the pup stays. If he is given too big an area, this will hinder your training efforts. Crate training is based on the fact that a dog does not like to soil his sleeping quarters, so it is ineffective to keep a pup in an area that is so big that he can eliminate in one end and get far enough away from it to sleep. Also, you want to make the crate den-like for the pup. Blankets and a favorite toy will make the crate cozy for the small pup; as he grows, you may want to evict some of his "roommates" to make more room. It will take some coaxing at first, but be patient. Given some time to get used to it, your pup will adapt to his new home-within-a-home quite nicely.

INTRODUCTION TO THE FAMILY

Everyone in the house will be excited about the puppy's coming home and will want to pet him and play with him, but it is best to make the introductions low-key so as not to overwhelm the puppy. He is apprehensive already. It is the first time he has been separated from his mother and the breeder, and the ride to your home is likely the first time he has been in a car. The last thing you want to do is smother him, as this will only frighten him further. This is not to say that human contact is not extremely necessary at this stage, because this is the time when a connection between the pup and his human family is formed. Gentle petting and soothing words should help console him, as well as just putting him down and letting him explore on his own (under your watchful eye, of course).

The pup may approach the family members or may busy himself with exploring for a while. Gradually, each person should spend some time with the pup, one at a time, crouching down to get as close to the pup's level as possible while letting him sniff their hands and petting him gently. The pup definitely needs human attention and he needs to be touched—this is how to form an immediate bond. Just remember that the pup is experiencing a lot of things for the first time, at the same time. There are new people, new noises, new smells and new things to investigate, so be gentle, be affectionate and be as comforting as you can be.

YOUR PUP'S FIRST NIGHT HOME

You have traveled home with your new charge safely in his crate or on a friend's lap. He's been to the vet for a thorough check-up; he's been weighed, his papers examined; perhaps he's even been vaccinated and wormed as well. He's met the whole family, including the excited children and the less-than-happy cat. He's explored his area, his new bed, the yard and anywhere else he's been permitted. He's eaten his first meal at home and relieved himself in the proper

During their time at the breeder's, the pups get used to spending all of their time, awake and asleep, with their littermates. Being part of a puppy pack is comforting to them, so be prepared to help your puppy overcome the shock of being separated from his siblings when he comes to your home.

place. He's heard lots of new sounds, smelled new friends and seen more of the outside world than ever before. That was just the first day! He's worn out and is ready for bed...or so you think!

It's puppy's first night home and you are ready to say "good night." Keep in mind that this is puppy's first night ever to be sleeping alone. His dam and litter-mates are no longer at paw's length and he's a bit scared, cold and lonely. Be reassuring to your new family member, but this is not the time to spoil him and give in to his inevitable whining.

Puppies whine. They whine to let the others know where they are and hopefully to get company out of it. Place your pup in his new bed or crate in this room and close the door. Mercifully, he may fall asleep without a peep. When the inevitable occurs, ignore the whining: he is fine. Be strong and keep his best interest in mind. Do not allow yourself to become guilty and visit the pup. He will fall asleep eventually.

Many breeders recommend

THE RIDE HOME

Taking your dog from the breeder to your home in a car can be a very uncomfortable experience for both of you. The puppy will have been taken from his warm, friendly, safe environ-ment and brought into a strange new environment—an environment that moves! Be prepared for loose bowels, urination, crying, whining and even fear biting. With proper love and encouragement when you arrive home, the stress of the trip should quickly disappear.

placing a piece of bedding from the pup's former home in his new bed so that he recognizes the scent of his littermates. Others still advise placing a hot-water bottle in his bed for warmth. The latter may be a good idea, provided the pup doesn't attempt to suckle—he'll get good and wet and may not fall asleep so fast.

Puppy's first night can be somewhat stressful for the pup and his new family. Remember that you are setting the tone of nighttime at your house. Unless you want to play with your pup every night at 10 p.m., midnight and 2 a.m., don't initiate the habit. Your family will thank you, and soon so will your pup!

PREVENTING PUPPY PROBLEMS

SOCIALIZATION
Now that you have done all of the preparatory work and have

PUP MEETS WORLD
Thorough socialization includes not only meeting new people but also being introduced to new experiences such as riding in the car, having his coat brushed, hearing the television, walking in a crowd—the list is endless. The more your pup experiences, and the more positive the experiences are, the less of a shock and the less frightening it will be for your pup to encounter new things.

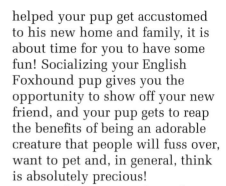

helped your pup get accustomed to his new home and family, it is about time for you to have some fun! Socializing your English Foxhound pup gives you the opportunity to show off your new friend, and your pup gets to reap the benefits of being an adorable creature that people will fuss over, want to pet and, in general, think is absolutely precious!

Besides getting to know his new family, your puppy should be exposed to other people, animals and situations, but he should not be exposed to dogs you don't know well until he has received the required vaccinations. Socialization will help your puppy become well adjusted as he grows up and less prone to being timid or fearful of the new things he will encounter. Your pup's socialization began at the breeder's, but now it is your responsibility to continue it. The socialization he receives up until the age of 12 weeks is the most critical, as this is the time when he forms his impressions of the outside world. Be especially careful during the eight-to-ten-week-old period, also known as the fear period. The interaction he receives during this time should be gentle and reassuring. Lack of socialization can manifest itself in fear and aggression as the dog grows up. He needs lots of human contact, affection, handling and exposure to other animals.

Once your pup has received his necessary vaccinations, feel free to take him out and about (on his lead, of course). Walk him around the neighborhood, take him on your daily errands, let people pet him, let him meet other dogs and pets, etc. Puppies do not have to try to make friends; there will be no shortage of people who will want to introduce themselves. Just make sure that you carefully supervise each meeting. If the neighborhood children want to say hello, for example, that is great—children and pups most often make great companions. However, sometimes an excited child can unintention-ally handle a pup too roughly, or an overzealous pup can playfully nip a little too hard. You want to make socialization experiences positive ones. What a pup learns during this very formative stage will impact his attitude toward future encounters, and you want your pup to grow up to be comfortable around everyone. A pup that has a bad experience with a child may grow up to be a dog that is shy around or aggres-sive toward children.

CONSISTENCY IN TRAINING

Dogs, being pack animals, naturally need a leader, or else they try to establish dominance in their packs. When you bring a dog into your family, the choice of who becomes the leader and who becomes the

pack is entirely up to you! Your pup's intuitive quest for dominance, coupled with the fact that it is nearly impossible to look at an adorable English Foxhound pup with his "puppy-dog" eyes and billowing ears and not cave in, give the pup almost an unfair advantage in getting the upper paw! A pup will definitely test the waters to see what he can and cannot do.

Do not give in to those pleading hound eyes—stand your ground when it comes to disciplining the pup and make sure that all family members do the same. It will only

MANNERS MATTER
During the socialization process, a puppy should meet people, experience different environments and definitely be exposed to other canines. Through playing and interacting with other dogs, your puppy will learn lessons, ranging from controlling the pressure of his jaws by biting his littermates to the inner-workings of the canine pack that he will apply to his relationships with humans and other dogs for the rest of his life. That is why removing a puppy from his litter too early (before eight weeks) can be detrimental to the pup's development.

CHEWING TIPS

Chewing goes hand in hand with nipping in the sense that a teething puppy is always looking for a way to soothe his aching gums. In this case, instead of chewing on you, he may have taken a liking to your favorite shoe or something else that he should not be chewing. Again, realize that this is a normal canine behavior that does not need to be discouraged, only redirected. Your pup just needs to be taught what is acceptable to chew on and what is off-limits. Consistently tell him "No!" when you catch him chewing on something forbidden and give him a chew toy.

Conversely, praise him when you catch him chewing on something appropriate. In this way, you are discouraging the inappropriate behavior and reinforcing the desired behavior. The puppy's chewing should stop after his adult teeth have come in, but an adult dog continues to chew for various reasons—perhaps because he is bored, needs to relieve tension or just likes to chew. That is why it is important to redirect his chewing when he is still young.

home…and be consistent in enforcing them! Early training shapes the dog's personality, so you cannot be unclear in what you expect.

COMMON PUPPY PROBLEMS
The best way to prevent puppy problems is to be proactive in stopping an undesirable behavior as soon as it starts. The old saying "You can't teach an old dog new tricks" does not necessarily hold true, but it *is* true that it is much easier to discourage bad behavior in a young developing pup than to wait until the pup's bad behavior becomes the adult dog's bad habit. There are some problems that are especially prevalent in puppies as they develop.

NIPPING
As puppies start to teethe, they feel the need to sink their teeth into anything available…unfortunately, that includes your fingers, arms, hair, and toes. You may find this behavior cute for the first five seconds…until you feel just how sharp those puppy teeth are. This is something you want to discourage immediately and consistently with a firm "No!" (or whatever number of firm "Nos" it takes for him to understand that you mean business). Then replace your finger with an appropriate chew toy. While this behavior is merely annoying when the dog is young, it can become dangerous

confuse the pup when Mother tells him to get off the couch when he is used to sitting up there with Father to watch the nightly news. Avoid discrepancies by having all members of the household decide on the rules before the pup even comes

as your English Foxhound's adult teeth grow in and his jaws develop if he continues to think it is okay to nibble on his human friends. Your English Foxhound does not mean any harm with a friendly nip, but he also does not know his own strength.

CRYING/WHINING

Your pup will often cry, whine, whimper, howl or make some type of commotion when he is left alone. This is basically his way of calling out for attention to make sure that you know he is there and that you have not forgotten about him. He feels insecure when he is left alone, when you are out of the house and he is in his crate or when you are in another part of the house and he cannot see you. The noise your puppy is making is an expression of the anxiety he feels at being alone, so he needs to be taught that being alone is okay. You are not actually training the dog to stop making noise, you are training him to feel comfortable when he is alone and thus removing the need for him to make the noise.

This is where the crate with a cozy blanket and a favorite toy comes in handy. You want to know that your pup is safe when you are not there to supervise, and you know that he will be safe in his crate rather than roaming freely about the house. In order for the pup to stay in his crate without making a fuss, he needs to be comfortable in his crate. On that note, it is extremely important that the crate is never used as a form of punishment, or the pup will develop a negative association with the crate.

Accustom the pup to the crate in short, gradually increasing time intervals in which you put him in the crate, maybe with a treat, and stay in the room with him. If he cries or makes a fuss, do not go to him, but stay in his sight. Gradually he will realize that staying in his crate is just fine without your help, and it will not be so traumatic for him when you are not around. You may want to leave the radio on softly when you leave the house; the sound of human voices may be comforting.

IN DUE TIME
It will take at least two weeks for your puppy to become accustomed to his new surroundings. Give him lots of love, attention, handling, frequent opportunities to relieve himself, a diet he likes to eat and a place he can call his own.

ENGLISH FOXHOUND

DIETARY AND FEEDING CONSIDERATIONS

You have probably heard it a thousand times: "You are what you eat." Believe it or not, it's very true. Dogs are what you feed them because they have little choice in the matter. Even those people who truly want to feed their dogs the best often have trouble doing so because they do not know which foods are best for their dog. Only by understanding their dogs' dietary needs can owners make informed decisions.

Dog foods are produced in three basic types: dry, semi-moist and canned. Dry foods are the choice of the cost-conscious because they are much less expensive than semi-moist and canned. Dry foods contain the least fat and the most preservatives. Most canned foods are 60–70% water, while semi-moist foods are so full of sugar that they are the least preferred by owners, though dogs welcome them (as a child does candy).

Three stages of development must be considered when selecting a food for your dog: the puppy stage, the adult stage and the senior stage.

STORING DOG FOOD

You must store your dry dog food carefully. Open packages of dog food quickly lose their vitamin value, usually within 90 days of being opened. Mold spores and vermin could also contaminate the food.

PUPPY STAGE

Puppies have a natural instinct to suck milk from their mother's teats. They exhibit this behavior from the first moments of their lives. If they don't suckle within a short while, the breeder must attempt to put them onto their mother's nipples, selecting ones with plenty of milk. A newborn's failure to suckle often requires the breeder to hand-feed the pup under the guidance of a veterinarian. This involves a baby bottle and a special formula. The mother's milk is much better than any formula, despite there being excellent formulas available, because it contains colostrum, a sort of antibiotic milk that protects the puppies during the first eight to ten weeks of their lives.

Puppies should be allowed to nurse from their mother for about the first six weeks, although, starting around the third or fourth week, the breeder will begin to introduce small portions of suitable solid food. Most breeders like to introduce alternate milk and meat meals initially, building up to weaning time.

By the time the puppies are seven or a maximum of eight weeks old, they should be fully weaned and fed solely on a proprietary puppy food. Selection of the most suitable, good-quality diet at this time is essential, for a puppy's fastest growth rate is during the first year of life. Large breeds like the English Foxhound must not be fed foods that encourage them to grow too rapidly; rather, the food should contain a proper balance to promote sound, stable growth. Your vet and breeder should be able to offer good advice in this regard.

FOOD PREFERENCE

Selecting the best dry dog food is difficult. There is no majority consensus among veterinary scientists as to the value of nutrient analysis (protein, fat, fiber, moisture, ash, cholesterol, minerals, etc.). All agree that feeding trials are what matter most, but you also have to consider the individual dog. The dog's weight, age and activity level, and what pleases his taste, all must be considered. It is probably best to take the advice of your veterinarian. Every dog has individual dietary requirements, and should be fed accordingly.

If your dog is fed a good dry food, he does not require supplements of meat or vegetables. Dogs do appreciate a little variety in their diets, so you may choose to stay with the same brand but vary the flavor. Alternatively, you may wish to add a little flavored stock to give a difference to the taste.

TEST FOR PROPER DIET
A good test for proper diet is the color, odor and firmness of your dog's stool. A healthy dog usually produces three semi-hard stools per day. The stools should have no unpleasant odor. They should be the same color from excretion to excretion.

The amount of food and the frequency of meals will change as the puppy grows up. The number of meals per day will be reduced as he matures. Puppies have very high energy levels, so they must be fed enough to gain weight properly and maintain a healthy weight. As a guideline for feeding, an English Foxhound pup can be fed four times a day until three months of age; then three meals per day, giving slightly larger portions, between three and six months of age; then, once the puppy has reached six months old, you can reduce the feedings to twice daily. Puppy and junior diets should be balanced for your dog's needs, and supplements of vitamins, minerals and protein should not be necessary unless advised by the vet. At one year of age, some owners feed only one meal per day. However, to guard against bloat, it is generally accepted that two smaller meals are better for the dog's digestion than one large portion.

ADULT DIETS
A dog is considered an adult when he has stopped growing in height and/or length. Do not consider the dog's weight when the decision is made to switch from a puppy diet to a adult-maintenance diet. An English Foxhound is fully mature around 15 months of age, though it often takes another 12 to 18 months for the dog to reach his peak as a performance animal. Again you should rely upon your veterinarian or breeder to recommend an acceptable maintenance diet. Major dog-food manufacturers specialize in this type of food and it is just necessary for you to select the one best suited to your dog's needs. Active dogs have different requirements than more sedentary dogs.

Once you find a good maintenance diet, keep in mind that the food is balanced nutritionally and

A Worthy Investment

Veterinary studies have proven that a balanced high-quality diet pays off in your dog's coat quality, behavior and activity level. Invest in premium brands for the maximum payoff with your dog.

Treats are wonderful motivators in training and to reward your dog for good behavior, but don't overdo it! Carrots, small pieces of cheese and bits of cooked chicken or hot dog are popular choices, and many dog-food manufacturers specialize in healthy dog biscuits.

that giving the dog "extras" can spoil this balance. It is never a good idea to give your dog "people" snack foods; sugar and starches are not good for dogs, and some foods, such as chocolate and onions, are actually toxic to dogs. Likewise, fatty and spicy foods should not be offered to your dog and, although it may be tempting to "throw your Foxhound a bone," many natural bones can be dangerous as they can easily split and splinter, possibly causing choking or internal damage.

SENIOR DIETS

As dogs get older, their metabolism changes. The older dog usually exercises less, moves more slowly and sleeps more. This change in lifestyle and physiological performance requires a change in diet. Since these changes take place slowly,

they might not be recognizable. What is easily recognizable is weight gain. By continuing to feed your dog an adult-maintenance diet when he is slowing down metabolically, your dog will gain weight. Obesity in an older dog compounds the health problems

CHANGE IN DIET

As your dog's caretaker, you know the importance of keeping his diet consistent, but sometimes when you run out of food or if you're on vacation, you have to make a change quickly. Some dogs will experience digestive problems, but most will not. If you are planning on changing your dog's menu, do so gradually to ensure that your dog will not have any problems. Over a period of four to five days, slowly add some new food to your dog's old food, increasing the percentage of new food each day.

that already accompany old age.

As your dog gets older, few of his organs will function up to par. The kidneys slow down and the intestines become less efficient. These age-related factors are best handled with a change in diet and a change in feeding schedule to give smaller portions that are more easily digested.

There is no single best diet for every older dog, and the age at which you make the switch depends on your individual dog. While many dogs do well on light or senior diets, other dogs do better on special premium diets such as lamb and rice. Be sensitive to your senior English Foxhound's diet, and this will help control other problems that may arise with your old friend.

WATER

Just as your dog needs proper nutrition from his food, water is an essential "nutrient" as well. Water keeps the dog's body properly hydrated and promotes normal function of the body's systems. During housebreaking, it is necessary to keep an eye on how much water your English Foxhound is drinking so that you will be able to predict when he will need to relieve himself, but he should have access to clean, fresh water at all times. Make sure that the dog's water bowl is clean and elevated, and change the water often.

FEEDING TIPS
- Dog food must be served at room temperature, neither too hot nor too cold. Fresh water, changed often and served in a clean bowl, is mandatory.
- Never feed your dog from the table while you are eating, and never feed your dog leftovers from your own meal. They usually contain too much fat and too much seasoning.
- Dogs must chew their food. Hard pellets are excellent; soups and stews are to be avoided.
- Don't add leftovers or any extras to commercial dog food. The normal food is usually balanced, and adding something extra destroys the balance.
- Except for age-related changes, dogs do not require dietary variations. They can be fed the same diet, day after day, without their becoming bored or ill.

THE CANINE GOURMET

Your dog does not prefer a fresh bone. Indeed, he wants it properly aged and, if given such a treat indoors, he is more likely to try to bury it in the carpet than he is to settle in for a good chew! If you have a yard, give him such delicacies outside and guide him to a place suitable for his "bone yard." He will carefully place the treasure in its earthy vault and seemingly forget about it. Trust me, his seeming distaste or lack of thanks for your thoughtfulness is not that at all. He will return in a few days to inspect the bone, perhaps to re-bury it, and when it is just right, he will relish it as much as you do that cooked-to-perfection steak. If he is in a concrete or bricked kennel run, he will be especially frustrated at the hopelessness of the situation. He will vacillate between ignoring it completely, giving it a few licks to speed the curing process with saliva, and trying to hide it behind the water bowl! When the bone has aged a bit, he will set to work on it.

EXERCISE

All dogs require some form of exercise, regardless of breed. A sedentary lifestyle is as harmful to a dog as it is to a person. The English Foxhound happens to be an above-average breed when it comes to activity and energy; thus, he requires more exercise than most breeds. Regular walks, play sessions in the fenced yard or letting the dog run free in the yard or another secure enclosure under your supervision are all sufficient forms of exercise for the English Foxhound. For those who are more ambitious, you will find that your adult English Foxhound will be able to keep up with you on extra-long walks or your morning jogs, making your dog's exercise enjoyable and healthy for both of you!

Remember the English Foxhound's original purpose, and the physical endurance for which he is bred, and you will understand why your dog requires vigorous daily exercise to stay healthy and content. This is a very active breed that welcomes outdoor physical activity and plenty of it. Puppies, however, should not be permitted to overdo it. During their first year, when their growth plates are still forming and their joints are most vulnerable, refrain from exercise that involves impact on their front and rear legs.

Brisk walks, once the puppy reaches three or four months of age, will stimulate heart rates and build muscle for both dog and owner. As the dog reaches adulthood, the speed and distance of the walks can be increased as long as they are both kept reasonable and comfortable for both of you.

If you are interested in pursuing hunting with your Foxhound, he will revel in the strenuous activity of the hunt and the opportunity to use his innate skills. To get started, contact the national or local hunt clubs to find organizations in your area that promote hunting events for

Exercise is even better when it comes in the form of an activity with his beloved master. Daily walks are healthy for dog and owner, not to mention the benefits of time spent together!

TIPPING THE SCALES

Good nutrition is vital to your dog's health, but many people end up over-feeding or giving unnecessary supplements. Here are some common doggie diet don'ts:

- Adding milk, yogurt and cheese to your dog's diet may seem like a good idea for coat and skin care, but dairy products are very fattening and can cause indigestion.
- Diets high in fat will not cause heart attacks in dogs but will certainly cause your dog to gain weight.
- Most importantly, don't assume your dog will simply stop eating once he doesn't need any more food. Given the chance, he will eat you out of house and home!

the Foxhound breeds.

Some things to keep in mind regarding exercising your dog: First, exercise should be restricted for *at least* an hour before and two hours after mealtimes. Second, an overweight dog should never be suddenly over-exercised. Instead, he should be encouraged to increase exercise slowly. Finally, not only is exercise essential to keep the dog's body fit, it is essential to his mental well-being. A bored dog will find something to do, which often manifests itself in some type of destructive behavior. In this sense, exercise is just as essential for the owner's mental well-being!

Most hounds, including the English Foxhound, require very little grooming. Their coats can be kept in good condition by a weekly brushing or grooming with a hound glove, removing dead hair and debris and promoting a healthy shine.

GROOMING

BRUSHING

A natural bristle brush or a hound glove can be used for regular routine brushing. Weekly brushing is effective for removing dead hair and stimulating the dog's natural oils to add shine and a healthy look to the coat. Although the English Foxhound's coat is short and close, it does require these regular once-overs to keep it looking its shiny best. If your Foxhound picks up debris in his coat during his outdoor expeditions, an additional quick brush-through as needed will remove any foreign objects from his coat.

Aside from maintaining the dog's healthy coat, regular grooming sessions are also a good way to spend time with your dog. Many dogs grow to like the feel of being brushed and will enjoy the daily routine.

BATHING

Dogs do not need to be bathed as often as humans, but occasional bathing is essential for healthy skin and a clean, shiny coat. Again, like most anything, if you accustom your pup to being bathed as a puppy, it will be second nature by the time he grows up. You want your dog to be at ease in the bath or else it could end up a wet, soapy, messy ordeal for both of you!

EXERCISE ALERT!
You should be careful where you exercise your dog. Many areas have been sprayed with chemicals that are highly toxic to both dogs and humans. Never allow your dog to eat grass or drink from puddles on either public or private grounds, as the run-off water may contain chemicals from sprays and herbicides.

Brush your English Foxhound thoroughly before wetting his coat. This will remove most dead hair. Make sure that your dog has a good non-slip surface to stand on. Begin by wetting the dog's coat. A shower or hose attachment is necessary for thoroughly wetting and rinsing the coat. Check the water temperature to make sure that it is neither too hot nor too cold.

Next, apply shampoo to the dog's coat and work it into a good lather. You should purchase a shampoo that is made for dogs. Do not use a product made for human hair; these are too harsh for use on dogs. Wash the head last; you do not want shampoo to drip into the dog's eyes while you are washing the rest of his body. Work the shampoo all the way down to the skin. You can use this opportunity to check the skin for any bumps, bites or other abnormalities. Do not neglect any area of the body—get all of the

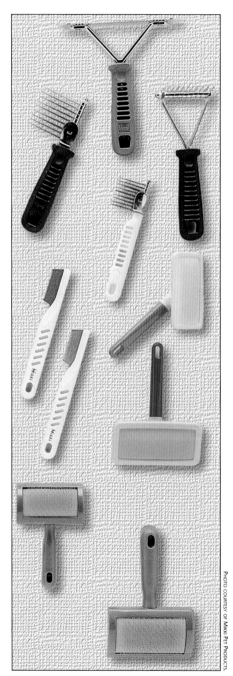

hard-to-reach places.

Once the dog has been thoroughly shampooed, he requires an equally thorough rinsing. Shampoo left in the coat can be irritating to the skin. Protect his eyes from the shampoo by shielding them with your hand and directing the flow of water in the opposite direction. You should also avoid getting water in the ear canal. Be prepared for your dog to shake out his coat—you might want to stand back, but make sure you have a hold on the dog to keep him from running through the house, and have a heavy towel ready to dry him off.

EAR CLEANING

The ears should be kept clean and any excess hair inside the ear should be trimmed. Ears can be cleaned with a cotton ball and special liquid cleaner or ear powder made for dogs. Avoid using cotton swabs, as these pose a risk of probing into the dog's ear canal, something you never should do. While cleaning your English Foxhound's ears, be on the lookout for any signs of infection or ear-mite infestation. If your English Foxhound has been shaking his head or scratching at his ears frequently, this usually indicates a problem. If his ears have an unusual odor, this is a sure sign of mite infestation or infection, and a signal to have his ears checked by the veterinarian.

NAIL CLIPPING

Your English Foxhound should be accustomed to having his nails trimmed at an early age since it will be a part of your maintenance routine throughout his life. Not only does it look nicer, but a dog with long nails can cause harm if he scratches someone unintentionally. Also, a long nail has a better chance of ripping and bleeding, or of causing the feet to spread. A good rule of thumb is that if you can hear your dog's nails' clicking on the floor when he walks, his nails are too long.

Before you start cutting, make sure you can identify the "quick" in each nail. The quick is a blood vessel that runs through the center of each nail and grows rather close to the end. It will bleed if accidentally cut, which will be quite painful for the dog as it contains nerve endings. Keep some type of clotting agent on hand, such as a styptic pencil or styptic powder (the type used for shaving). This will stop the bleeding quickly when applied to the end of the cut nail. Do not panic if this happens, just stop the bleeding and talk soothingly to your dog. Once he has calmed down, move on to the next nail. It is better to clip a little at a time, particularly with dark-nailed dogs.

Hold your pup steady as you begin trimming his nails; you do not want him to make any sudden

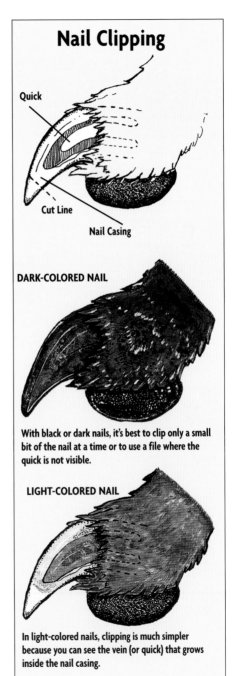

Nail Clipping

Quick

Cut Line

Nail Casing

DARK-COLORED NAIL

With black or dark nails, it's best to clip only a small bit of the nail at a time or to use a file where the quick is not visible.

LIGHT-COLORED NAIL

In light-colored nails, clipping is much simpler because you can see the vein (or quick) that grows inside the nail casing.

movements or run away. Talk to him soothingly and stroke his fur as you clip. Holding his foot in your hand, simply take off the end of each nail in one quick clip. You can purchase nail clippers that are specially made for dogs; you can probably find them wherever you buy pet supplies. Many owners find those of the guillotine type easiest to use.

PEDICURE TIP

A dog that spends a lot of time outside on a hard surface, such as cement or pavement, will have his nails naturally worn down and may not need to have them trimmed as often, except maybe in the colder months when he is not outside as much. Regardless, it is best to get your dog accustomed to the nail-trimming procedure at an early age so that he is used to it. Some dogs are especially sensitive about having their feet touched, but if a dog has experienced it since puppyhood, it should not bother him.

TRAVELING WITH YOUR DOG

CAR TRAVEL

You should accustom your English Foxhound to riding in a car at an early age. You may or may not take him for rides in the car often, but at the very least he will need to go to the vet and you do not want these trips to be traumatic for the dog or a big hassle for you. The safest way for a dog to ride in the car is in his crate. If he uses a crate in the house, you can use the same crate for travel. If not, you should purchase an appropriately sized travel crate.

Put the pup in the crate and see how he reacts. If he seems

uneasy, you can have a passenger hold him on his lap while you drive; of course, this will only be an option when your Foxhound is very young. Another option is a specially made safety harness for dogs, which straps the dog in much like a seat belt. Do not let the dog roam loose in the vehicle—this is very dangerous! If you should stop short, your dog can be thrown and injured. If the dog starts climbing on you and pestering you while you are driving, you will not be able to concentrate on the road. It is an unsafe situation for everyone—human and canine.

For long trips, bring along some water and be prepared to

DEADLY DECAY
Did you know that periodontal disease (a condition of the bone and gums surrounding a tooth) can be fatal? Making dental-care at home part of your grooming routine and having your dog's teeth and mouth checked yearly can prevent it.

Your English Foxhound should never be allowed to roam free in the car while you are driving. If you have an SUV, station wagon or similar-type vehicle, you can partition the back section of the vehicle to create a safe area for your dog. Special gates are made specifically for this purpose.

stop to let the dog relieve himself; be sure to keep him on-lead during stops to prevent him from "hunting" around. Also bring along whatever you need to clean up after him. You should bring along some old towels and rags in case he has a potty accident in the car or suffers from motion sickness.

AIR TRAVEL
Contact your chosen airline before proceeding with travel plans that include your English Foxhound. The dog will be required to travel in a fiberglass crate and you should always check in advance

with the airline regarding specific requirements for the crate's size, type and labeling, as well as any travel restrictions or necessary health certificates.

To help put the dog at ease for the flight, make sure he is accustomed to his travel crate beforehand and give him one of his favorite toys in the crate. Do not feed your English Foxhound for several hours prior to checking in so that you minimize his need to relieve himself. Some airlines require you to provide documentation as to when the dog was last fed. In any case, a light meal is best. For long trips, you will have to attach food and water bowls to the outside of your dog's crate so that airline employees can tend to him between legs of the trip.

Make sure that your dog is properly identified and that your contact information appears on his ID tags and on his crate. Your English Foxhound will travel in a different area of the plane than the human passengers, so every rule must be strictly followed to prevent any risk of getting separated from your dog.

VACATIONS AND BOARDING

So you want to take a family vacation and you want to include *all* members of the family. You would probably make arrange-

IDENTIFICATION OPTIONS

As puppies become more and more expensive, especially those puppies of high quality for showing and/or breeding, they have a greater chance of being stolen. The usual collar dog tag is, of course, easily removed. But there are two more permanent techniques that have become widely used for identification.

The puppy microchip implantation involves the injection of a small microchip, about the size of a corn kernel, under the skin of the dog. If your dog shows up at a clinic or shelter, or is offered for resale under less-than-savory circumstances, he can be positively identified by the microchip. The microchip is scanned, and a registry quickly identifies you as the owner.

Tattooing is done on various parts of the dog, from his belly to his ears. The number tattooed can be your telephone number, your dog's registration number or any other number that you can easily memorize. When professional dog thieves see a tattooed dog, they usually lose interest. For the safety of our dogs, no laboratory facility or dog broker will accept a tattooed dog as stock.

Discuss microchipping and tattooing with your veterinarian and breeder. Some vets perform these services on their own premises for a reasonable fee. To ensure that your dog's identification is effective, be certain that the dog is then properly registered with a legitimate national database.

ments for accommodations ahead of time anyway, but this is especially important when traveling with a dog. You do not want to make an overnight stop at the only place around for miles and find out that they do not allow dogs. Also, you do not want to reserve a place for your family without confirming that you are traveling with a dog because, if it is against the hotel's policy, you may end up without a place to stay.

Alternatively, if you are traveling and choose not to bring your English Foxhound, you will have to make arrangements for him while you are away. Some options are to bring him to a friend's house to stay while you are gone, to have a trusted neighbor stop by often or stay at your house or to bring your dog to a reputable boarding kennel. If you choose to board him at a kennel, you should look at the kennels in your area to find one with which you are comfortable. Look at the facilities and where the dogs are kept to make sure that they are clean and of ample size. Talk to some of the employees and see how they treat the dogs—are they knowledgeable and attentive, do they spend time with the dogs, play with them, exercise them, etc.? You know that your English Foxhound will not be happy unless he gets regular activity. Also find out the

kennel's policy on vaccinations and what they require. This is for all of the dogs' safety, since when dogs are kept together, there is a greater risk of diseases being passed from dog to dog. Many veterinarians offer boarding facilities; this may be another option.

IDENTIFICATION

Your English Foxhound is your valued companion and friend. That is why you always keep a close eye on him and you have made sure that he cannot escape from the yard or wriggle out of his collar and run away from you. However, accidents can happen and there may come a time when your dog unexpectedly gets separated from you. If this unfortunate event should occur, the first thing on your mind will be finding him. Proper identification, including an ID tag and possibly a tattoo and/or a microchip, will increase the chances of his being returned to you safely and quickly.

Tattoos are becoming more and more common as a form of ID for dogs. It is not painful for the dog, and usually can be done by your vet. The light skin of the ear flap is a common place for a dog to be tattooed.

TRAINING YOUR
ENGLISH FOXHOUND

Living with an untrained dog is a lot like owning a piano that you do not know how to play—it is a nice object to look at, but it does not do much more than that to bring you pleasure. Now try taking piano lessons, and suddenly the piano comes alive and brings forth magical sounds and rhythms that set your heart singing and your body swaying.

The same is true with your English Foxhound. At first, you enjoy seeing him around the house. He does not do much with you other than to need food, water and "bathroom" trips. Come to think of it, he does not bring you

Preparing to train your Foxhound means arming yourself with plenty of patience and praise, a positive attitude and a pocketful of treats!

much joy, either. He is a big responsibility with a very small return. Often he develops unacceptable behaviors that annoy and/or frustrate you, to say nothing of bad habits that may end up costing you great sums of money. Not a good thing!

Now train your English Foxhound. Enroll in an obedience class. Teach your dog good manners as you learn how and why he behaves the way he does. Find out how to communicate with your dog and how to recognize and understand his communications with you. Suddenly the dog takes on a new role in your life—he is smart, interesting, well behaved and fun to be with. He demonstrates his bond of devotion to you daily. In

other words, your English Foxhound does wonders for your ego because he constantly reminds you that you are not only his leader, you are his hero! Miraculous things have happened—you have a wonderful dog (even your family and friends have noticed the transformation!) and you feel good about yourself.

Those involved with teaching dog obedience and counseling owners about their dogs' behavior have discovered some interesting facts about dog ownership. For example, training dogs when they are puppies results in the highest rate of success in developing well-mannered and well-adjusted adult dogs. Training an older dog, from six months to six years of age, can produce almost equal results, providing that the owner accepts the dog's slower rate of learning capability and is willing to work patiently to help the dog succeed at developing to his fullest potential. Unfortunately, many owners of untrained adult dogs lack the patience factor, so they do not persist until their dogs are successful at learning particular behaviors.

Training a puppy aged 8 to 16 weeks (20 weeks at the most) is like working with a dry sponge in a pool of water. The pup soaks up whatever you show him and constantly looks for more things to do and learn. At this early age, his body is not yet producing

REAP THE REWARDS

If you start with a normal, healthy dog and give him time, patience and some carefully executed lessons, you will reap the rewards of that training for the life of the dog. And what a life it will be! The two of you will find immeasurable pleasure in the companionship you have built together with love, respect and understanding.

hormones, and therein lies the reason for such a high rate of success. Without hormones, he is focused on his owners and not particularly interested in investigating other places, dogs, people,

CALM DOWN
Dogs will do anything for your attention. If you reward the dog when he is calm and attentive, you will develop a well-mannered dog. If, on the other hand, you greet your dog excitedly and encourage him to wrestle with you, the dog will greet you the same way and you will have a hyperactive dog on your hands.

etc. You are his leader: his provider of food, water, shelter and security. He latches onto you and wants to stay close. He will usually follow you from room to room, will not let you out of his sight when you are outdoors with him and will respond in like manner to the people and animals you encounter. If you greet a friend warmly, he will be happy to greet the person as well. If, however, you are hesitant or anxious about the approach of a stranger, he will respond accordingly to you.

Once the puppy begins to produce hormones, his natural curiosity emerges and he begins to investigate the world around him. It is at this time when you may notice that the untrained dog begins to wander away from you and even ignore your commands to stay close. When this behavior becomes a problem, you have two choices: get rid of the dog or train him. It is strongly urged that you choose the latter option.

Occasionally, there will be no obedience classes available within a reasonable distance from your home. Sometimes there are classes available, but the tuition is too costly. Whatever the circumstances, the solution to training your English Foxhound without formal obedience lessons lies within the pages of this book.

This chapter is devoted to helping you train your English

A fenced yard is the most convenient place in which to housebreak your Foxhound.

Foxhound at home. If the recommended procedures are followed faithfully, you may expect positive results that will prove rewarding to both you and your dog. Whether your new charge is a puppy or a mature adult, the methods of teaching and the techniques we use in training basic behaviors are the same. After all, no dog of any breed, whether puppy or adult, likes harsh or inhumane methods. All creatures, however, respond favorably to gentle motivational methods and sincere praise and encouragement. Now let us get started.

HOUSEBREAKING

You can train a puppy to relieve himself wherever you choose. For example, city dwellers often train their puppies to relieve themselves along the curbside because large plots of grass are not readily available. Suburbanites, on the other hand, usually have yards to accommodate their dogs' needs, which will usually be the case with English Foxhounds.

Outdoor training includes such surfaces as grass, dirt and cement. Indoor training usually means training your dog to newspaper, although this is not a viable option for owners of large dogs like the English Foxhound. When deciding on the surface and location that you will want your English Foxhound to use, be sure it is going to be permanent. Training your dog to grass and then changing your mind two months later is extremely difficult for both you and the dog.

are not fully developed. Therefore, like human babies, puppies need to relieve themselves frequently.

Take your puppy out often—every hour for an eight-week-old, for example. The older the puppy, the less often he will need to relieve himself. Finally, as a mature healthy adult, he will require only three to five relief trips per day.

HOUSING
Since the types of housing and control you provide for your puppy have a direct relationship on the success of house-training, we consider the various aspects of both before we begin training. Bringing a new puppy home and turning him loose in your house can be compared to turning a child loose in an amusement park and telling the child that the place

Living room, bedroom, bathroom...it's one and the same to young pups who have not yet learned to relieve themselves outside their quarters. Many breeders line their litters' areas with clean absorbent material.

Next, choose the command you will use each and every time you want your puppy to relieve himself. "Hurry up" and "Let's go" are examples of commands commonly used by dog owners. Get in the habit of asking the puppy, "Do you want to go hurry up?" (or whatever your chosen relief command is) before you take him out. That way, when he becomes an adult, you will be able to determine if he wants to go out when you ask him. A confirmation will be signs of interest such as wagging his tail, watching you intently, going to the door, etc.

PUPPY'S NEEDS
Your puppy needs to relieve himself after play periods, after each meal, after he has been sleeping and any time he indicates that he is looking for a place to urinate or defecate. The urinary and intestinal tract muscles of very young puppies

THE CLEAN LIFE
By providing sleeping and resting quarters that fit the dog, and offering frequent opportunities to relieve himself outside his quarters, the puppy quickly learns that the outdoors is the place to go when he needs to urinate or defecate. It also reinforces his innate desire to keep his sleeping quarters clean. This, in turn, helps develop the muscle control that will eventually produce a dog with clean living habits.

is all his! The sheer enormity of the place would be too much for him to handle.

Instead, offer the puppy clearly defined areas where he can play, sleep, eat and live. A room of the house where the family gathers is the most obvious choice. Puppies are social animals and need to feel a part of the pack right from the start. Hearing your voice, watching you while you are doing things and smelling you nearby are all positive reinforcers that he is now a member of your pack. Usually a family room, the kitchen or a nearby adjoining breakfast nook is ideal for providing safety and security for both puppy and owner.

Within that room, there should be a smaller area that the puppy can call his own. A wire or fiberglass dog crate or a partitioned-off (not boarded!) corner from which he can view the activities of his new family will be fine. The size of the area or crate is the key factor here. The area must be large enough for the puppy to lie down and stretch out as well as stand up without rubbing his head on the top, yet small enough so that he cannot relieve himself at one end and sleep at the other without coming into contact with his droppings. Dogs are, by nature, clean animals and will not remain close to their relief areas unless forced to do so. In those cases, they then become

dirty dogs and usually remain that way for life.

The crate or area should be lined with clean bedding and the pup can be offered one toy, no more. Avoid putting food or water in the crate during the house-training process, as eating and drinking will activate the pup's digestive processes and ultimately defeat your purpose as well as make the puppy very uncomfortable as he attempts to "hold it." Once he is reliably trained, water should be made available at all times, in a non-spill container.

TAKE THE LEAD

Do not carry your dog to his relief area. Lead him there on a leash or, better yet, encourage him to follow you to the spot. If you start carrying him to his spot, you might end up doing this routine forever and your dog will have the satisfaction of having trained *you*.

PAPER CAPER

Never line your pup's sleeping area with newspaper. Puppy litters are usually raised on newspaper and, once in your home, the puppy will immediately associate newspaper with voiding. Never put newspaper on any floor while house-training, as this will only confuse the puppy. Finally, restrict water intake after evening meals. Offer a few licks at a time—never let a Foxhound of any age gulp water after meals.

CONTROL

By *control*, we mean helping the puppy to create a lifestyle pattern that will be compatible to that of his human pack (you!). Just as we guide little children to learn our way of life, we must show the puppy when it is time to play, eat, sleep, exercise and even entertain himself. Your puppy should always sleep in his crate. He should also learn that, during times of household confusion and excessive human activity such as at breakfast when family members are preparing for the day, he can play by himself in relative safety and comfort in his crate. Each time you leave the puppy alone, he should be crated.

Puppies are chewers. They cannot tell the difference between things like lamp cords, television wires, shoes, table legs, etc. Chewing into a television wire, for example, can be fatal to the puppy, while a shorted wire can start a fire in the house. In another example, if the puppy chews on the arm of the chair when he is alone, you would probably discipline him angrily when you get home. Thus, he makes the association that your coming home means he is going to be scolded or punished. (He would not remember chewing up the chair and is incapable of making the association of the discipline with his naughty deed.) Acclimating the pup to his

CANINE DEVELOPMENT SCHEDULE

It is important to understand how and at what age a puppy develops into adulthood. If you are a puppy owner, consult the following Canine Development Schedule to determine the stage of development your puppy is currently experiencing. This knowledge will help you as you work with the puppy in the weeks and months ahead.

Period	Age	Characteristics
FIRST TO THIRD	**BIRTH TO SEVEN WEEKS**	Puppy needs food, sleep and warmth, and responds to simple and gentle touching. Needs mother for security and disciplining. Needs littermates for learning and interacting with other dogs. Pup learns to function within a pack and learns pack order of dominance. Begin socializing pup with adults and children for short periods. Pup begins to become aware of his environment.
FOURTH	**EIGHT TO TWELVE WEEKS**	Brain is fully developed. Pup needs socializing with outside world. Remove from mother and littermates. Needs to change from canine pack to human pack. Human dominance necessary. Fear period occurs between 8 and 12 weeks. Avoid fright and pain.
FIFTH	**THIRTEEN TO SIXTEEN WEEKS**	Training and formal obedience should begin. Less association with other dogs, more with people, places, situations. Period will pass easily if you remember this is pup's change-to-adolescence time. Be firm and fair. Flight instinct prominent. Permissiveness and over-disciplining can do permanent damage. Praise for good behavior.
JUVENILE	**FOUR TO EIGHT MONTHS**	Another fear period about 7 to 8 months of age. It passes quickly, but be cautious of fright and pain. Sexual maturity reached. Dominant traits established. Dog should understand sit, down, come and stay by now.

NOTE: THESE ARE APPROXIMATE TIME FRAMES. ALLOW FOR INDIVIDUAL DIFFERENCES IN PUPPIES.

designated area not only keeps him safe but also avoids his engaging in destructive behaviors when you are not around.

Times of excitement, such as family parties, holidays, friends' visits, etc., can be fun for the puppy, providing he can view the activities from the security of his crate. He is not underfoot and he is not being fed all sorts of tidbits that will probably cause him stomach distress, yet he still feels a part of the fun.

Dogs use their sensitive noses to gain important information like which dogs have been there before, where's the best place to go to the bathroom and other pertinent details of dogdom.

KEEP SMILING
Never train your dog, puppy or adult, when you are angry or in a sour mood. Dogs are very sensitive to human feelings, especially anger, and if your dog senses that you are angry or upset, he will connect your anger with his training and learn to resent or fear his training sessions.

ESTABLISHING A SCHEDULE
Your puppy should be taken to his relief area each time he is released from his crate, after meals, after play sessions and when he first awakens in the morning (at age eight weeks, this can mean 5 a.m.!). The puppy will indicate that he's ready "to go" by circling or sniffing busily—do not misinterpret these signs. For a puppy less than ten weeks of age, a routine of taking him out every hour is necessary. As the puppy grows, he will be able to wait for longer periods of time.

Keep trips to his relief area short. Stay no more than five or six minutes and then return to the house. If he goes during that time, praise him lavishly and take him indoors immediately. If he does not, but he has an accident when you go back indoors, pick him up immediately, say "No! No!" and return to his relief area. Wait a few minutes, then return to the house again. Never hit a puppy or put his face in urine or excrement when he has an accident!

Once indoors, put the puppy in his crate until you have had time to clean up his accident. Then release him to the family area and watch him more closely than before. Chances are, his accident was a result of your not picking up his signal or waiting too long before offering him the opportunity to relieve himself. Never hold a grudge against the puppy for accidents.

Let the puppy learn that going outdoors means it is time to relieve himself, not to play. Once trained, he will be able to play indoors and out and still differentiate between the times for play versus the times for relief. Help him develop regular hours for naps, being alone, playing by himself and just resting, all in his crate. Encourage him to entertain himself while you are busy with your activities. Let him learn that having you near is comforting, but it is not your main purpose in life to provide him with undivided attention.

Each time you put your puppy in his crate, tell him "Crate time!" (or whatever command you choose). Soon, he will run to his crate when he hears you say those words. In the beginning of his training, do not leave him in his crate for prolonged periods of time except during the night when everyone is sleeping. Make his experience with his crate a

HOW MANY TIMES A DAY?

AGE	RELIEF TRIPS
To 14 weeks	10
14–22 weeks	8
22–32 weeks	6
Adulthood (dog stops growing)	4

These are estimates, of course, but they are a guide to the *minimum* number of opportunities a dog should have each day to relieve himself.

pleasant one and, as an adult, he will love his crate and willingly stay in it for several hours at a time. The dogs accept this as their lifestyle and look forward to "crate time."

Crate training provides safety for you, the puppy and the home. It also provides the puppy with a feeling of security, and that helps the puppy achieve self-confidence and clean habits. Remember that one of the primary ingredients in house-training your puppy is control. Regardless of your lifestyle, there will always be occasions when you will need to have a place where your dog can stay and be happy and safe. Crate training is the answer for now and in the future.

In conclusion, a few key elements are really all you need for a successful house-training method—consistency, frequency, praise, control and supervision.

THE SUCCESS METHOD

Success that comes by luck is usually short-lived. Success that comes by well-thought-out proven methods is often more easily achieved and permanent. This is the Success Method. It is designed to give you, the puppy owner, a simple yet proven way to help your puppy develop clean living habits and a feeling of security in his new environment.

6 Steps to Successful Crate Training

1 Tell the puppy "Crate time!" and place him in the crate with a small treat (a piece of cheese or half of a biscuit). Let him stay in the crate for five minutes while you are in the same room. Then release him and praise lavishly. Never release him when he is fussing. Wait until he is quiet before you let him out.

2 Repeat Step 1 several times a day.

3 The next day, place the puppy in the crate as before. Let him stay there for ten minutes. Do this several times.

4 Continue building time in five-minute increments until the puppy stays in his crate for 30 minutes with you in the room. Always take him to his relief area after prolonged periods in his crate.

5 Now go back to Step 1 and let the puppy stay in his crate for five minutes, this time while you are out of the room.

6 Once again, build crate time in five-minute increments with you out of the room. When the puppy will stay willingly in his crate (he may even fall asleep!) for 30 minutes with you out of the room, he will be ready to stay in it for several hours at a time.

By following these procedures with a normal, healthy puppy, you and the puppy will soon be past the stage of "accidents" and ready to move on to a clean and rewarding life together.

ROLES OF DISCIPLINE, REWARD AND PUNISHMENT

Discipline, training one to act in accordance with rules, brings order to life. It is as simple as that. Without discipline, particularly in a group society, chaos reigns supreme and the group will eventually perish. Humans and canines are social animals and need some form of discipline in order to function effectively. They must procure food, reproduce to keep their species going and

protect their home base and their young.

If there were no discipline in the lives of social animals, they would eventually die from starvation and/or predation by other stronger animals. In the case of domestic canines, dogs need discipline in their lives in order to understand how their pack (you and other family members) functions and how they must act in order to survive.

A large humane society in a highly populated area recently surveyed dog owners regarding their satisfaction with their relationships with their dogs. People who had trained their dogs were 75% more satisfied with their pets than those who had never trained their dogs.

Noted psychologist Dr. Edward Thorndike established *Thorndike's Theory of Learning*, which states that a behavior that

To a dog, nothing says "a job well done" like his owner's attention and affection. Show your Foxhound when you approve of his behavior.

> ### PRACTICE MAKES PERFECT!
> • Have training lessons with your dog every day in several short segments—three to five times a day for a few minutes at a time is ideal.
> • Do not have long practice sessions. The dog will become easily bored.
> • Never practice when you are tired, ill, worried or in an otherwise negative mood. This will transmit to the dog and may have an adverse effect on his performance.
>   Think fun, short and above all *positive!* End each session on a high note, rather than a failed exercise, and make sure to give a lot of praise. Enjoy the training and help your dog enjoy it, too.

necessary. The best type of punishment often comes from an outside source. For example, a child is told not to touch the stove because he may get burned. He disobeys and touches the stove. In doing so, he receives a burn. From that time on, he respects the heat of the stove and avoids contact with it. Therefore, a behavior that results in an unpleasant event tends not to be repeated.

A good example of a dog's learning the hard way is the dog who chases the house cat. He is told many times to leave the cat alone, yet he persists in teasing the cat. Then, one day he begins chasing the cat but the cat turns and swipes a claw across the dog's face, leaving him with a painful gash on his nose. The final result is that the dog stops chasing the cat.

Have a sturdy collar and lead, comfortable for the dog to wear and for you to handle, for your training sessions.

results in a pleasant event tends to be repeated. A behavior that results in an unpleasant event, similarly, tends not to be repeated. It is this theory on which training methods are based today. For example, if you manipulate a dog to perform a specific behavior and reward him for doing it, he is likely to do it again because he enjoyed the end result.

Occasionally, punishment, a penalty inflicted for an offense, is

TRAINING EQUIPMENT

COLLAR AND LEAD
For the English Foxhound, the collar and lead that you use for training must be one with which you are easily able to work, not too heavy for the dog and perfectly safe. A simple buckle collar is fine for most dogs. One who pulls mightily on the lead may require a choke collar (correctly used by an educated owner) in the beginning of training.

TREATS

Have a bag of treats on hand. Something nutritious and easy to swallow works best. Use a soft treat, a chunk of cheese or a piece of cooked chicken rather than a dry biscuit. By the time the dog finishes chewing a dry treat, he will forget why he is being rewarded in the first place!

In training, rewarding the dog with a food treat will help him associate praise and the treats with learning new behaviors that obviously please his owner. Using food rewards will not teach a dog to beg at the table—the only way to teach a dog to beg at the table is to give him food from the table.

TRAINING BEGINS: ASK THE DOG A QUESTION

In order to teach your dog anything, you must first get his attention. After all, he cannot learn anything if he is looking away from you with his mind on something else.

To get his attention, ask him "School?" and immediately walk over to him and give him a treat as you tell him "Good dog." Wait a minute or two and repeat the routine, this time with a treat in your hand as you approach within a foot of the dog. Do not go directly to him, but stop about a foot short of him and hold out the treat as you ask "School?" He will see you approaching with a treat in your hand and most

PLAN TO PLAY

Your Foxhound should also have regular play and exercise sessions when he is with you or a family member. Exercise for a very young puppy can consist of a short walk around the house or yard. Playing can include fetching games with a large ball or a special toy, or retrieving games in which the dog brings objects to you. Remember to restrict play periods to indoors within his living area (the family room, for example) until he is completely house-trained. Outdoor play should take place in securely enclosed areas.

likely begin walking toward you. As you meet, give him the treat and praise again.

The third time, ask the question, have a treat in your hand and walk only a short distance toward the dog so that he must walk almost all the way to you. As he reaches you, give him the treat and praise again. By this time, the dog will probably be getting the idea that if he pays attention to you, especially when you ask that question, it will pay off in treats and fun activities for him. In other words, he learns that "school" means doing fun things with you that result in treats and positive attention for him.

Remember that the dog does not understand your verbal language; he only recognizes sounds. Your question translates to a series of sounds for him, and those sounds become the signal to go to you and pay attention; if he does, he will get to interact with you plus receive treats and praise.

Take time to talk to your dog! Dogs are intuitive creatures that tune in to their owners' tone of voice and body language. They respond well to positive attention... don't you?

> ## LANGUAGE BARRIER
> Dogs do not understand our language and have to rely on tone of voice more than just words or sound. They can be trained to react to a certain sound, at a certain volume. If you say "No, Oliver" in a very soft, pleasant voice, it will not have the same meaning as "No, Oliver!!" when you raise your voice.
>
> You should never use the dog's name during a reprimand, just the command "No! " You never want the dog to associate his name with a negative experience or reprimand.

THE BASIC COMMANDS

TEACHING SIT

Now that you have the dog's attention, attach his lead and hold it in your left hand and a food treat in your right. Place your food hand at the dog's nose and let him lick the treat but not take it from you. Say "Sit" and slowly raise your food hand from in front of the dog's nose up over his head so that he is looking at the ceiling. As he bends his head upward, he will have to bend his knees to maintain his balance. As he bends his knees, he will assume a sit position. At that point, release the food treat and praise lavishly with comments such as "Good dog! Good sit!" Remember to always praise enthusiastically, because dogs relish verbal praise from their owners and feel so proud of themselves whenever they accomplish a behavior.

Incidentally, you will not use food forever in getting the dog to obey your commands. Food is only used to teach new behaviors, and once the dog knows what you want when you give a specific command, you will wean him off the food treats but still maintain the verbal praise. After all, you will always have your voice with you, and there will be many times when you have no food rewards but expect the dog to obey.

TEACHING DOWN

Teaching the down exercise is easy when you understand how the dog perceives the down position, and it is very difficult when you do not. Dogs perceive the down position as a submissive one; therefore, teaching the down exercise using a forceful method can sometimes make the dog develop such a fear of the down that he either runs away when you say "Down" or he attempts to bite the person who tries to force him down.

Have the dog sit close alongside your left leg, facing in the same direction as you are. Hold the lead in your left hand and a food treat in your right. Now place your left hand lightly on the top of the dog's shoulders

READY, SIT, GO!

On your marks, get set: train! Most professional trainers agree that the sit command is the place to start your dog's formal education. Sitting is a natural posture for most dogs and they respond to the sit exercise willingly and readily. For every lesson, begin with the sit command so that you start out on a successful note. Likewise, you should practice the sit command at the end of every lesson as well because you always want to end on a high note.

where they meet above the spinal cord. Do not push down on the dog's shoulders; simply rest your left hand there so you can guide the dog to lie down close to your left leg rather than to swing away from your side when he drops.

Now place the food hand at the dog's nose, say "Down" very softly (almost a whisper) and slowly lower the food hand to the dog's front feet. When the

food hand reaches the floor, begin moving it forward along the floor in front of the dog. Keep talking softly to the dog, saying things like, "Do you want this treat? You can do this, good dog." Your reassuring tone of voice will help calm the dog as he tries to follow the food hand in order to get the treat.

When the dog's elbows touch the floor, release the food and praise softly. Try to get the dog to maintain that down position for several seconds before you let him sit up again. The goal here is to get the dog to settle down and not feel threatened in the down position.

TEACHING STAY

It is easy to teach the dog to stay in either a sit or a down position. Again, we use food and praise during the teaching process as we help the dog to understand exactly what it is that we are expecting him to do.

To teach the sit/stay, start with the dog sitting on your left side as before and hold the lead in your left hand. Have a food treat in your right hand and place your food hand at the dog's nose. Say "Stay" and step out on your right foot to stand directly in front of the dog, toe to toe, as he licks and nibbles the treat. Be sure to keep his head facing upward to maintain the sit position. Count to five and then

---

DOUBLE JEOPARDY

A dog in jeopardy never lies down. He stays alert on his feet because instinct tells him that he may have to run away or fight for his survival. Therefore, if a dog feels threatened or anxious, he will not lie down. Consequently, it is important to keep the dog calm and relaxed as he learns the down exercise.

swing around to stand next to the dog again with him on your left. As soon as you get back to the original position, release the food and praise lavishly.

To teach the down/stay, do the down as previously described. As soon as the dog lies down, say "Stay" and step out on your right foot just as you did in the sit/stay. Count to five and then return to stand beside the dog with him on your left side. Release the treat and praise as always.

Within a week or ten days, you can begin to add a bit of distance between you and your dog when you leave him. When you do, use your left hand open with the palm facing the dog as a stay signal, much the same as the hand signal a police officer uses to stop traffic at an intersection. Hold the food treat in your right hand as before, but this time the food is not touching the dog's nose. He will watch the food hand and quickly learn that he is going to get that treat as soon as you return to his side.

When you can stand 3 feet away from your dog for 30 seconds, you can then begin building time and distance in both stays. Eventually, the dog can be expected to remain in the stay position for prolonged periods of time until you return to him or call him to you. Always praise lavishly when he stays.

TEACHING COME

If you make teaching "come" a fun experience, you should never have a student that does not love the game or that fails to come when called. The secret, it seems, is never to teach the word "come."

At times when an owner most wants his dog to come when

In the sit/stay, the hand gesture along with your verbal command signals for the dog to stay while you increase the distance between the two of you.

CONSISTENCY PAYS OFF

Dogs need consistency in their feeding schedule, exercise and relief visits, and in the verbal commands you use. If you use "Stay" on Monday and "Stay here, please" on Tuesday, you will confuse your dog. Don't demand perfect behavior during training sessions and then let him have the run of the house the rest of the day. Above all, lavish praise on your pet consistently every time he does something right. The more he feels he is pleasing you, the more willing he will be to learn.

A few turns of the "Where are you?" game and the dog will figure out that everyone is playing the game and that each person has a big celebration awaiting the dog's success at locating him. Once the dog learns to love the game, simply calling out "Where are you?" will bring him running from wherever he is when he hears that all-important question.

The come command is recognized as one of the most important things to teach a dog, but there are trainers who work with thousands of dogs and never teach the actual word "come." Yet these dogs will race to respond to a person who uses the dog's name followed by "Where are you?" For example, a woman has a 12-year-old companion dog who went blind, but who never fails to locate her owner when asked, "Where are you?"

Children particularly love to play this game with their dogs. Children can hide in smaller

"Here I come!" You always want your Foxhound to respond eagerly to your call.

called, the owner is likely upset or anxious and he allows these feelings to come through in the tone of his voice when he calls his dog. Hearing that desperation in his owner's voice, the dog fears the results of going to him and therefore either disobeys outright or runs in the opposite direction. The secret, therefore, is to teach the dog a game and, when you want him to come to you, simply play the game. It is practically a no-fail solution!

To begin, have several members of your family take a few food treats and each go into a different room in the house. Take turns calling the dog, and each person should celebrate the dog's finding him with a treat and lots of happy praise. When a person calls the dog, he is actually inviting the dog to find him and get a treat as a reward for "winning."

"COME" . . . BACK

Never call your dog to come to you for a correction or scold him when he reaches you. That is the quickest way to turn a come command into "Go away fast!" Dogs think only in the present tense, and your dog will connect the scolding with coming to you, not with the misbehavior of a few moments earlier.

places like a shower or bathtub, behind a bed or under a table. The dog needs to work a little bit harder to find these hiding places, but, when he does, he loves to celebrate with a treat and a tussle with a favorite youngster.

TEACHING HEEL

Heeling means that the dog walks beside the owner without pulling. It takes time and patience on the owner's part to succeed at teaching the dog that he (the owner) will not proceed unless the dog is walking calmly beside him. Pulling out ahead on the lead is definitely not acceptable.

Begin with holding the lead in your left hand as the dog sits beside your left leg. Move the loop end of the lead to your right hand but keep your left hand short on the lead so it keeps the dog in close next to you.

Say "Heel" and step forward on your left foot. Keep the dog close to you and take three steps. Stop and have the dog sit next to you in what we now call the heel position. Praise verbally, but do not touch the dog. Hesitate a moment and begin again with "Heel," taking three steps and stopping, at which point the dog is told to sit again.

Your goal here is to have the dog walk those three steps without pulling on the lead. When he will walk calmly beside you for three steps without

pulling, increase the number of steps you take to five. When he will walk politely beside you while you take five steps, you can increase the length of your walk to ten steps. Keep increasing the length of your stroll until the dog will walk quietly beside you without pulling as long as you want him to heel. When you stop

HEELING WELL

Teach your dog to heel in an enclosed area. Once you think the dog will obey reliably and you want to attempt advanced obedience exercises such as off-lead heeling, test him in a fenced-in area so he cannot run away.

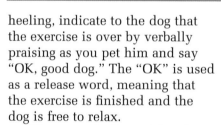

FEAR AGGRESSION

Pups who are subjected to physical abuse during training commonly end up with behavioral problems as adults. One common result of abuse is fear aggression, in which a dog will lash out, bare his teeth, snarl and finally bite someone by whom he feels threatened. For example, your daughter may be playing with the dog one afternoon. As they play hide-and-seek, she backs the dog into a corner and, as she attempts to tease him playfully, he bites her hand. Examine the cause of this behavior. Did your daughter ever hit the dog? Did someone who resembles your daughter hit or scream at the dog?

Fortunately, fear aggression is relatively easy to correct. Have your daughter engage in only positive activities with the dog, such as feeding, petting and walking. She should not give any corrections or negative feedback. If the dog still growls or cowers away from her, allow someone else to accompany them. After approximately one week, the dog should feel that he can rely on her for many positive things, and he will also be prevented from reacting fearfully towards anyone who might resemble her.

heeling, indicate to the dog that the exercise is over by verbally praising as you pet him and say "OK, good dog." The "OK" is used as a release word, meaning that the exercise is finished and the dog is free to relax.

If you are dealing with a dog who insists on pulling you around, simply "put on your brakes" and stand your ground until the dog realizes that the two of you are not going anywhere until he is beside you and moving at your pace, not his. It may take some time just standing there to convince the dog that you are the leader and you will be the one to decide on the direction and speed of your travel.

Each time the dog looks up at you or slows down to give a slack lead between the two of you, quietly praise him and say, "Good

heel. Good dog." Eventually, the dog will begin to respond and within a few days he will be walking politely beside you without pulling on the lead. At first, the training sessions should be kept short and very positive; soon the dog will be able to walk nicely with you for increasingly longer distances. Remember also to give the dog free time and the opportunity to run and play when you are done with heel practice.

WEANING OFF FOOD IN TRAINING

Food is used in training new behaviors. Once the dog understands what behavior goes with a specific command, it is time to start weaning him off the food treats. At first, give a treat after each exercise. Then, start to give a treat only after every other exercise. Mix up the times when you offer a food reward and the times when you offer only praise so that the dog will never know when he is going to receive both food and praise and when he is going to receive only praise. This is called a variable-ratio reward system and it proves successful because there is always the chance that the owner will produce a treat, so the dog never stops trying for that reward. No matter what, *always* give verbal praise.

OBEDIENCE CLASSES

As previously discussed, it is a good idea to enroll in an obedience class if one is available in your area. If yours is a potential show dog, classes to prepare for the show ring would be appropriate. Many areas have dog clubs that offer basic obedience training as well as preparatory classes for obedience competition. There are also local dog trainers who offer similar classes.

At obedience trials, dogs can earn titles at various levels of competition. The beginning levels of competition include basic behaviors such as sit, down, heel, etc. The more advanced levels of competition include jumping, retrieving, scent discrimination and signal work. The advanced levels require a dog and owner to put a lot of time and effort into their training. The titles that can be earned at these levels of competition are very prestigious.

Showing classes build confidence for both dog and handler, giving you and your Foxhound the assurance to present yourselves in the best manner possible when it's your turn to enter the ring.

SAFETY FIRST
While it may seem that the most important things to your dog are eating, sleeping and chewing the upholstery on your furniture, his first concern is actually safety. The domesticated dogs we keep as companions have the same pack instinct as their ancestors who ran free thousands of years ago. Because of this pack instinct, your dog wants to know that he and his pack are not in danger of being harmed, and that his pack has a strong, capable leader. You must establish yourself as the leader early on in your relationship. That way, your dog will trust that you will take care of him and the pack, and he will accept your commands without question.

THE STUDENT'S STRESS TEST

During training sessions, you must be able to recognize signs of stress in your dog such as:

- tucking his tail between his legs
- lowering his head
- shivering or trembling
- standing completely still or running away
- panting and/or salivating
- avoiding eye contact
- flattening his ears back
- urinating submissively
- rolling over and lifting a leg
- grinning or baring teeth
- aggression when restrained

If your four-legged student displays these signs, he may just be nervous or intimidated. The training session may have been too lengthy, with not enough praise and affirmation. Stop for the day and try again tomorrow.

OTHER ACTIVITIES FOR LIFE

Whether a dog is trained in the structured environment of a class or alone with his owner at home, there are many activities that can bring fun and rewards to both owner and dog once they have mastered basic control. Teaching the dog to help out around the home, in the yard or on the farm provides great satisfaction to both dog and owner. In addition, the dog's help makes life a little easier for his owner and raises his stature as a valued companion to his family. It helps give the dog a purpose by occupying his mind and providing an outlet for his energy.

Backpacking is an exciting and healthful activity that the dog can be taught without assistance from more than his owner. The exercise of walking and climbing is good

"Thanks for being a great teacher!" Your Foxhound will appreciate the time and dedication you invest in his training, and you will appreciate having a well-behaved dog with whom it's a joy to spend time.

Those who share their lives with Foxhounds marvel in their dogs' intelligence and versatility, and treasure the companionship of this unique and wonderful breed.

for man and dog alike, and the bond that they develop together is priceless. The rule of thumb for backpacking with any dog is that the dog should never carry more than one-sixth of his body weight.

If you are interested in participating in organized competition with your English Foxhound, there are activities other than obedience in which you and your dog can become involved. Of course, the most obvious activity for the English Foxhound is hunting, and there are specialty clubs throughout the country that

sponsor competitive hunting events for Foxhounds. The active and athletic English Foxhound also can fare well in agility. In this popular and fun sport, dogs run through an obstacle course that includes various jumps, tunnels and other exercises to test the dog's speed and coordination. The owners run through the course beside their dogs to give commands and to guide them through the course. Although competitive, the focus is on fun— it's fun to do, fun to watch, and great exercise.

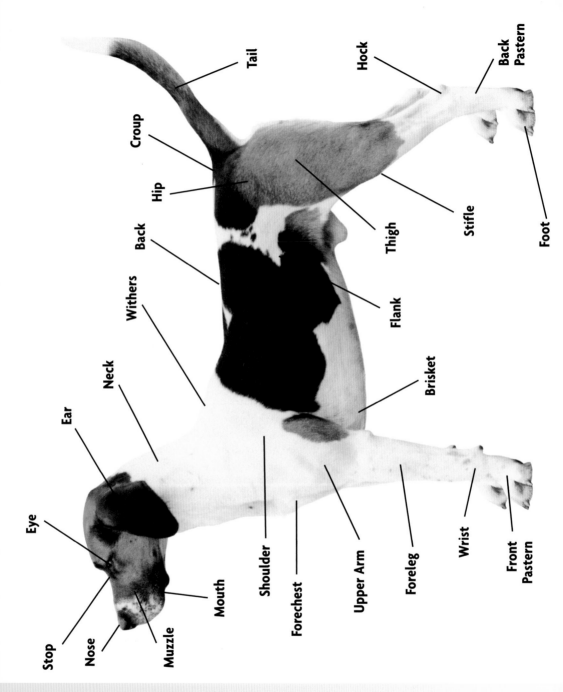

Physical Structure of the English Foxhound

ENGLISH FOXHOUND

Dogs suffer from many of the same physical illnesses as people. They might even share many of the same psychological problems. Since people usually know more about human diseases than canine maladies, many of the terms used in this chapter will be familiar but not necessarily those used by veterinarians. We will use the term *x-ray*, instead of the more acceptable term *radiograph*. We will also use the familiar term *symptoms* even though dogs don't have symptoms, which are verbal descriptions of the patient's feelings; instead, dogs have *clinical signs*. Since dogs can't speak, we have to look for clinical signs, but we still use the term *symptoms* in this book.

As a general rule, medicine is *practiced*. That term is not arbitrary. Medicine is a constantly changing art as we learn more and more about genetics, electronic aids (like CAT scans and MRI scans) and daily laboratory advances. There are many dog maladies, like canine hip dysplasia, which are not universally treated in the same manner. For example, some veterinarians opt for surgical treatments more often than others do.

SELECTING A VETERINARIAN
Your selection of a veterinarian should be based upon personality and skills with dogs, especially Foxhounds or similar breeds if possible, as well as upon convenience to your home. You want a vet who is close because you might have emergencies or need to make multiple visits for treatments. You want a vet who has services that you might require such as a boarding kennel and tattooing, who is current on the latest medical developments and advances and who has a good reputation for ability and responsiveness. There is nothing more frustrating than having to wait a day or more to get a response from your veterinarian.

All veterinarians are licensed and should be capable of dealing with routine medical issues such as regular exams, infections, injuries, the promotion of health (for example, by vaccination) and routine surgeries (such as neutering/spaying, stitching up wounds, etc). There are, however, many veterinary specialties that require further studies and internships. These include specialists in heart problems (veterinary cardiologists), skin

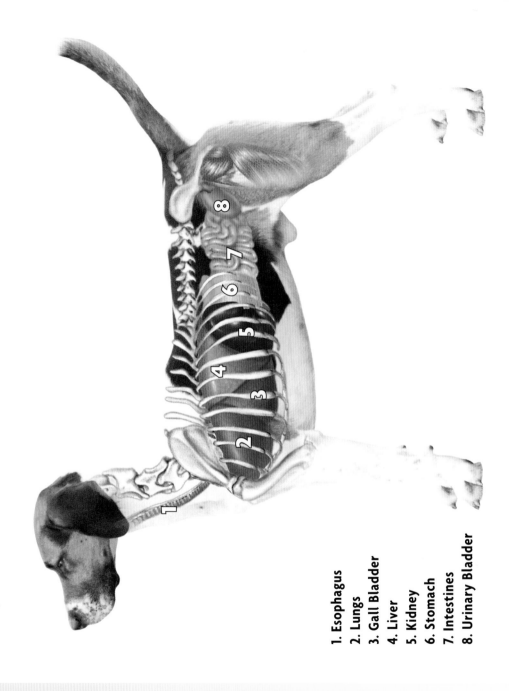

1. Esophagus
2. Lungs
3. Gall Bladder
4. Liver
5. Kidney
6. Stomach
7. Intestines
8. Urinary Bladder

Internal Organs of the English Foxhound

problems (veterinary dermatologists), tooth and gum problems (veterinary dentists), eye problems (veterinary ophthalmologists) and x-rays (veterinary radiologists), and surgeons who have specialties in bones, muscles or certain organs. If your dog requires the attention of a specialist, your vet will refer you to someone in the relevant field.

When the problem affecting your dog is serious, it is not unusual or impudent to get another medical opinion, although it is courteous to advise the vets concerned that you are doing so. You might also want to compare costs among several veterinarians. Sophisticated health care and veterinary services can be very costly. Don't be bashful about discussing these costs with your veterinarian. If there is more than one treatment option, it is not infrequent that financial considerations may play a role in deciding which route to take. You may also want to explore veterinary insurance policies, which are becoming more common and popular.

PREVENTATIVE MEDICINE
It is much easier, less costly and more effective to practice preventative medicine than to fight bouts of illness and disease. Properly bred puppies come from parents that were selected based upon their genetic-disease profiles.

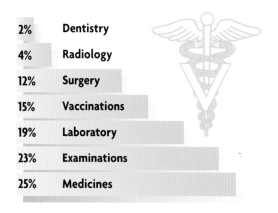

Breakdown of Veterinary Income by Category

%	Category
2%	Dentistry
4%	Radiology
12%	Surgery
15%	Vaccinations
19%	Laboratory
23%	Examinations
25%	Medicines

A typical vet's income, categorized according to services performed. This survey dealt with small-animal (pets) practices.

Their mother should have been vaccinated, free of all internal and external parasites and properly nourished. For these reasons, a visit to the veterinarian who cared for the dam is recommended. The dam can pass on disease resistance to her puppies, which can last for eight to ten weeks. She can also pass on parasites and many infections. That's why it's important to know as much about her health as possible.

WEANING TO BRINGING PUPPY HOME
Puppies should be weaned by the time they are about two months old. A puppy that remains for at least eight weeks with his mother and littermates usually adapts better to other dogs and people later in life.

You should have your newly acquired puppy examined by a

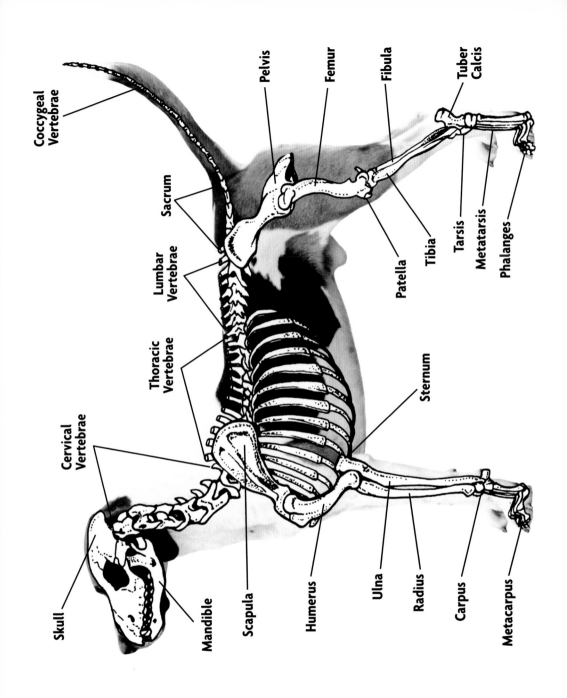

Skeletal Structure of the English Foxhound

veterinarian immediately; ideally, before bringing him home, unless he is overtired by the journey home from the breeder's. In that case, an appointment should be made for the next day.

The puppy will have his teeth examined and his skeletal conformation and general health checked prior to certification by the veterinarian. Many puppies have problems with their kneecaps, cataracts and other eye problems, heart murmurs and undescended testicles. Your veterinarian also might have training in temperament evaluation. At the first visit, your vet will set up a schedule for the puppy's vaccinations.

VACCINATION SCHEDULING
Most vaccinations are given by injection and should only be done by a veterinarian. Both he and you should keep a record of the date of the injection, the identification of the vaccine and the amount given. The first vaccination should start when the puppy is 6–8 weeks old, the second when he is 10–12 weeks of age and the third when he is 14–16 weeks of age. Vaccination scheduling is usually based on a two- to four-week cycle.

HEALTH AND VACCINATION SCHEDULE

AGE IN WEEKS:	6TH	8TH	10TH	12TH	14TH	16TH	20-24TH	52ND
Worm Control	✔	✔	✔	✔	✔	✔	✔	
Neutering							✔	
Heartworm		✔		✔		✔	✔	
Parvovirus	✔		✔		✔		✔	✔
Distemper		✔		✔		✔		✔
Hepatitis		✔		✔		✔		✔
Leptospirosis								✔
Parainfluenza	✔		✔		✔			✔
Dental Examination		✔					✔	✔
Complete Physical		✔					✔	✔
Coronavirus				✔			✔	✔
Canine Cough	✔							
Hip Dysplasia							✔	
Rabies							✔	

Vaccinations are not instantly effective. It takes about two weeks for the dog's immune system to develop antibodies. Most vaccinations require annual booster shots. Your vet should guide you in this regard.

Normal hairs of a dog, enlarged 200 times original size. The cuticle (outer covering) is clean and healthy. Unlike human hair that grows from the base, a dog's hair also grows from the end. Damaged hairs and split ends, illustrated above.

SCANNING ELECTRON MICROGRAPHS BY DR. DENNIS KUNKEL, UNIVERSITY OF HAWAII.

Most vaccinations immunize your puppy against viruses. The usual vaccines contain immunizing doses of several different viruses such as distemper, parvovirus, parainfluenza and hepatitis. There are other vaccines available when the puppy is at risk. You should rely upon professional advice. This is especially true for the booster-shot program. Most vaccination programs require a booster when the puppy is a year old and once a year thereafter. In some cases, circumstances may require more or less frequent immunizations.

Canine cough, more formally known as tracheobronchitis, is treated with a vaccine that is sprayed into the dog's nostrils. This is often included as part of the routine vaccinations, but the vaccine for canine cough often is not as effective as the vaccines for other major diseases.

FIVE MONTHS TO ONE YEAR OF AGE
By the time your puppy is five months old, he should have completed his vaccination program. During his physical

examination, he should be evaluated for the common hip dysplasia and other diseases of the joints. There are tests to assist in the prediction of these problems. Other tests can be run to assess the effectiveness of the vaccination program.

Unless you intend to breed or show your dog, neutering (male) or spaying (female) the puppy around six months of age is recommended. Discuss this with your veterinarian, who will explain all aspects of the procedure. Neutering and spaying

have proven to be extremely beneficial to both male and female dogs. Besides eliminating the possibility of pregnancy and pyometra in bitches and testicular cancer in males, it greatly reduces the risk of (but does not prevent) breast cancer in bitches and prostate cancer in male dogs.

Your vet should provide your puppy with a thorough dental evaluation at six months of age, ascertaining whether all of the permanent teeth have erupted properly. A home dental-care regimen should be initiated at six

DISEASE REFERENCE CHART

	What is it?	What causes it?	Symptoms
Leptospirosis	Severe disease that affects the internal organs; can be spread to people.	A bacterium, which is often carried by rodents, that enters through mucous membranes and spreads quickly throughout the body.	Range from fever, vomiting and loss of appetite in less severe cases to shock, irreversible kidney damage and possibly death in most severe cases.
Rabies	Potentially deadly virus that infects warm-blooded mammals.	Bite from a carrier of the virus, mainly wild animals.	1st stage: dog exhibits change in behavior, fear. 2nd stage: dog's behavior becomes more aggressive. 3rd stage: loss of coordination, trouble with bodily functions.
Parvovirus	Highly contagious virus, potentially deadly.	Ingestion of the virus, which is usually spread through the feces of infected dogs.	Most common: severe diarrhea. Also vomiting, fatigue, lack of appetite.
Canine cough	Contagious respiratory infection.	Combination of types of bacteria and virus. Most common: *Bordetella bronchiseptica* bacteria and parainfluenza virus.	Chronic cough.
Distemper	Disease primarily affecting respiratory and nervous system.	Virus that is related to the human measles virus.	Mild symptoms such as fever, lack of appetite and mucus secretion progress to evidence of brain damage, "hard pad."
Hepatitis	Virus primarily affecting the liver.	Canine adenovirus type I (CAV-1). Enters system when dog breathes in particles.	Lesser symptoms include listlessness, diarrhea, vomiting. More severe symptoms include "blue-eye" (clumps of virus in eye).
Coronavirus	Virus resulting in digestive problems.	Virus is spread through infected dog's feces.	Stomach upset evidenced by lack of appetite, vomiting, diarrhea.

months, including brushing weekly and providing good dental devices (such as hard plastic or nylon bones). Regular dental care promotes healthy teeth, fresh breath and a longer life.

DOGS OLDER THAN ONE YEAR

Continue to visit the veterinarian at least once a year. There is no such disease as old age, but bodily functions do change with age. The eyes and ears are no longer as efficient. Liver, kidney and intestinal functions often decline as the dog gets older. Proper dietary changes, recommended by your veterinarian, can make life more pleasant for the aging English Foxhound and you.

SKIN PROBLEMS IN ENGLISH FOXHOUNDS

Veterinarians are consulted by dog owners for skin problems more than for any other group of diseases or maladies. Dogs' skin is almost as sensitive as human skin, and both can suffer from almost the same ailments (though the occurrence of acne in most dogs is rare). For this reason, veterinary dermatology has developed into a specialty practiced by many veterinarians.

Since many skin problems have visual symptoms that are almost identical, it requires the skill of an experienced veterinary dermatologist to identify and cure many of the more severe skin disorders. Pet shops sell many treatments for skin problems, but most of the treatments are directed at symptoms and not the underlying problem(s). If your dog is suffering from a skin disorder, you should seek professional assistance as quickly as possible. As with all diseases, the earlier a problem is identified and treated, the more likely it is that the cure will be successful.

HEREDITARY SKIN DISORDERS

Veterinary dermatologists are currently researching a number of skin disorders that are believed to have hereditary bases. These inherited diseases are transmitted by both parents, who appear (phenotypically) normal but have a recessive gene for the disease, meaning that they carry, but are not affected by, the disease. These diseases pose serious problems to breeders because in some instances there are no methods of identifying carriers. Often the secondary diseases associated with these skin conditions are even more debilitating than the skin disorders themselves, including cancers and respiratory problems.

Among the hereditary skin disorders, for which the mode of inheritance is known, are acrodermatitis, cutaneous asthenia (Ehlers-Danlos syndrome), sebaceous adenitis, cyclic hematopoiesis, dermatomyositis, IgA deficiency, color dilution alopecia and nodular dermatofibrosis. Some of these disorders are limited to one or two breeds, while others affect a large number of breeds. All inherited diseases must be diagnosed and treated by a veterinary specialist.

PARASITE BITES

Many of us are allergic to mosquito bites. The bites itch, erupt and may even become infected. Dogs have the same reaction to fleas, ticks and/or mites. When you feel the prick of the mosquito as it bites you, you have a chance to kill it with your hand. Unfortunately, when your dog is bitten by a flea, tick or mite, he can only scratch it away or bite it. By the time the dog has been bitten, the parasite has done some of its damage. It may also have laid eggs to cause further problems in the near future. The itching from parasite bites is probably due to the saliva injected into the site when the parasite sucks the dog's blood.

AIRBORNE ALLLERGIES

Just as humans have hay fever, rose fever and other fevers from which they suffer during the pollinating season, many dogs suffer from the same allergies. When the pollen count is high, your dog might suffer, but don't expect him to sneeze and have a runny nose like a human would. Dogs react to pollen allergies the same way they react to fleas—they scratch and bite themselves. Dogs that spend a lot of time outdoors, like English Foxhounds, can be very susceptible to airborne pollen allergies.

Dogs, like humans, can be tested for allergens. Discuss the testing with your veterinary dermatologist.

ACRAL LICK GRANULOMA

Many large dogs have a very poorly understood syndrome called acral lick granuloma. The manifestation of the problem is the dog's tireless attack at a specific area of the body, almost always the

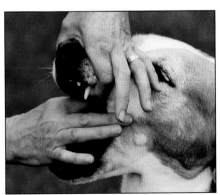

Getting a dog to swallow a pill can be quite a challange! Placing the pill at the back of the mouth and then stroking the throat to encourage the dog to swallow is a good method.

legs or paws. The dog licks so intensively that he removes the hair and skin, leaving an ugly, large wound. Tiny protuberances, which are outgrowths of new capillaries, bead on the surface of the wound. Owners who notice their dogs' biting and chewing at their extremities should have the vet determine the cause. If lick granuloma is identified, although there is no absolute cure, cortico-steroids are the most common treatment.

AUTO-IMMUNE ILLNESSES

An auto-immune illness is one in which the immune system overacts and does not recognize parts of the affected person; rather, the immune system starts to react as if these parts were foreign and need to be destroyed. An example is rheumatoid arthritis, which occurs when the body does not recognize the joints, thus leading to a very painful and damaging reaction in the joints. This has nothing to do with age, so can occur in children and young dogs. The wear-and-tear arthritis of the older person or dog is osteoarthritis.

Lupus is an auto-immune disease that affects dogs as well as people. It can take variable forms, affecting the kidneys, bones and the skin. It can be fatal, so is treated with steroids, which can themselves have very significant side effects. The steroids calm down the allergic reaction to the body's tissues, which helps the lupus, but the steroids also calm down the body's reaction to real foreign substances such as bacteria.

FOOD ALLERGIES

Dogs can be allergic to many foods that are best-sellers and highly recommended by breeders and veterinarians. Changing the brand of food that you buy may not eliminate the problem if the element to which the dog is allergic is contained in the new brand.

Recognizing a food allergy is difficult. Humans vomit or have rashes when we eat a food to which we are allergic. Dogs neither vomit nor (usually) develop a rash. They react in the same manner as they do to an airborne or flea allergy—they itch, scratch and bite, thus making the diagnosis extremely difficult. While pollen allergies and parasite bites are usually seasonal, food allergies are year-round problems.

FOOD INTOLERANCE

Food intolerance is the inability of the dog to completely digest certain foods. For example, puppies that may have done very well on their mother's milk may not do well on cow's milk. The results of food intolerance may be loose bowels, passing gas and stomach pains. These are the only obvious symptoms of food intoler-

HOW TO PREVENT BLOAT
Research has confirmed that the structure of deep-chested breeds contributes to their predisposition to bloat. Nevertheless, there are simple precautions that you can take to reduce the risk of this condition:
• Feed your dog twice daily rather than offer one big meal.
• Do not exercise your dog for at least one hour before and two hours after he has eaten.
• Make certain that your dog is calm and not overly excited while he is eating. It has been proven that nervous or overly excited dogs are more prone to develop bloat.
• Add a small portion of moist meat product to his dry food ration.
• Serve his meals and water in elevated bowl stands, which avoids craning his neck and swallowing air.
• To prevent your dog from gobbling his food too quickly, and thereby swallowing air, put some large (unswallowable) toys in his bowl so that he will have to eat around them to get his food.
• *Never* allow him to gulp water, especially at mealtimes.

ance and that makes diagnosis difficult since those signs can be symptomatic of various other problems as well.

TREATING FOOD PROBLEMS
It is possible to handle food allergies and food intolerance yourself. Put your dog on a diet that he has never had. Obviously, if he has never eaten this new food, he can't yet have been allergic or intolerant of it. Start with a single ingredient that is not in the dog's diet at the present time. Ingredients like chopped beef or chicken are common in dog's diets, so try something different like fish, lamb or another quality source of animal protein. Keep the dog on this diet (with no additives) for a month. If the symptoms of food allergy or intolerance disappear, chances are your dog has a food allergy.

Don't think that the single ingredient cured the problem. You still must find a suitable diet and ascertain which ingredient in the old diet was objectionable. This is most easily done by adding ingredients to the new diet one at a time. Let the dog stay on the modified diet for a month before you add another ingredient. Eventually, you will determine the ingredient that caused the adverse reaction.

An alternative method is to carefully study the ingredients in the diet to which your dog is allergic or intolerable. Identify the main ingredient in this diet and eliminate the main ingredient by buying a different food that does not have that ingredient. Keep experimenting until the symptoms disappear after one month on the new diet.

BLOAT OR GASTRIC TORSION
Bloat is a very dangerous problem that is found mainly in the large, deep-chested breeds. It

(Left) Cross-section through an English Foxhound, showing how deep the body cavity is. The muscles around the vertebrae give strength to the back.

(Right) The stomach hangs like a handbag with both straps broken within this deep body cavity. Support is provided by the junction with the esophagus and the junction with the duodenum.

Muscles around vertebrae

Abdominal cavity

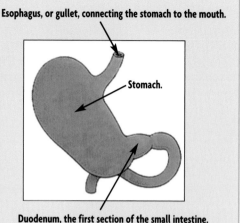

Esophagus, or gullet, connecting the stomach to the mouth.

Stomach.

Duodenum, the first section of the small intestine.

is the subject of much research, but still manages to take away many dogs before their time, in a very horrible way.

In order to understand how bloat affects the dog's stomach, let's first talk about the two ways in which the stomach is held in place. First, there is support provided by the junction with the esophagus, or gullet, and there is support provided by the junction with the first part of the small intestine; these make up the "broken straps of the handbag." The second, and the only other,

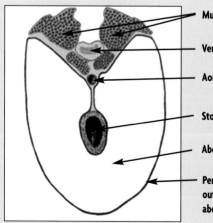

A second cross-section, showing support of the stomach provided by the peritoneum. This is the only source of support aside from that provided by the esophagus and duodenum.

Muscles around the vertebra.

Vertebra.

Aorta, the main blood vessel from the heart.

Stomach.

Abdominal cavity.

Peritoneum, the thin membrane lining the outside of the stomach and the inside of the abdominal cavity.

source of support is a thin layer of partially opaque "internal skin" called the peritoneum.

By looking at the illustrations, it's easy to see how the stomach can move around easily. Those breeds with the deepest chests are at the greatest risk of having their whole stomachs twist around (gastric torsion). This cuts off the blood supply and prevents the stomach's contents from leaving, and increases the amount of gas in the stomach. Once these things have happened, surgery is vital. If the blood supply has been cut off too long and a bit of the stomach wall dies, death of the English Foxhound is almost inevitable.

The horrendous pain of this condition is due to the stomach wall's being stretched by the gas caught in the stomach, as well as the stomach wall's desperately needing the blood that cannot get to it. There is the pain of not being able to pass a much greater than normal amount of wind; added to this is a pain equivalent to that of a heart attack, which is due to the heart muscle's being starved of blood.

It is possible for a dog to have more than one incident of gastric torsion, even if he has had his stomach stapled, in which case the stomach is stapled to the inside of the chest wall to give extra support and prevent its twisting.

DETECTING BLOAT
As important as it is to take precautions against bloat/gastric torsion, it is of equal importance to recognize the symptoms. It is necessary for your English Foxhound to get immediate veterinary attention if you notice any of the following signs:
- Your dog's stomach starts to distend, ending up large and as tight as a football;
- Your dog is dribbling, as no saliva can be swallowed;
- Your dog makes frequent attempts to vomit but cannot bring anything up due to the stomach's being closed off;
- Your dog is distressed from pain;
- Your dog starts to suffer from clinical shock, meaning that there is not enough blood in the dog's circulation as the hard, dilated stomach stops the blood from returning to the heart to be pumped around the body. Clinical shock is indicated by pale gums and tongue, as they have been starved of blood. The shocked dog also has glazed, staring eyes.

You have minutes—yes, *minutes*—to get your dog into surgery. If you see any of these symptoms at any time of the day or night, get to the vet immediately. Someone will have to phone and warn that you are on your way (which is a justification for the invention of the cellular phone!), so that they can be prepared to get your pet on the operating table right away.

A male dog flea, *Ctenocephalides canis.*

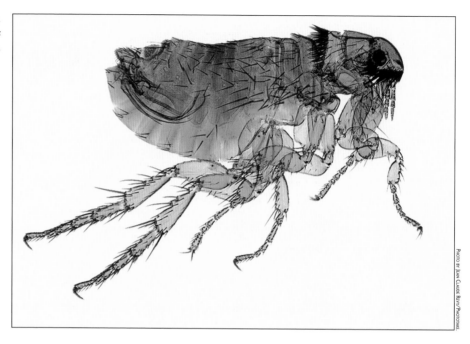

PHOTO BY JEAN CLAUDE REVY/PHOTOTAKE

EXTERNAL PARASITES

FLEAS

Of all the problems to which dogs are prone, none is more well known and frustrating than fleas. Flea infestation is relatively simple to cure but difficult to prevent. Parasites that are harbored inside the body are a bit more difficult to eradicate but they are easier to control.

To control flea infestation, you have to understand the flea's life cycle. Fleas are often thought of as a summertime problem, but centrally heated homes have changed the patterns and fleas can be found at any time of the year. The most effective method of flea control is a two-stage approach: one stage to kill the adult fleas, and the other to control the development of pre-adult fleas. Unfortunately, no single active ingredient is effective against all stages of the life cycle.

FLEA KILLER CAUTION— "POISON"

Flea-killers are poisonous. You should not spray these toxic chemicals on areas of a dog's body that he licks, including his genitals and his face. Flea killers taken internally are a better answer, but check with your vet in case internal therapy is not advised for your dog.

LIFE CYCLE STAGES

During its life, a flea will pass through four life stages: egg, larva, pupa or nymph and adult. The adult stage is the most visible and irritating stage of the flea life cycle, and this is why the majority of flea-control products concentrate on this stage. The fact is that adult fleas account for only 1% of the total flea population, and the other 99% exist in pre-adult stages, i.e., eggs, larvae and nymphs. The pre-adult stages are barely visible to the naked eye.

THE LIFE CYCLE OF THE FLEA

Eggs are laid on the dog, usually in quantities of about 20 or 30, several times a day. The adult female flea must have a blood meal before each egg-laying session. When first laid, the eggs will cling to the dog's hair, as the eggs are still moist. However, they will quickly dry out and fall from the dog, especially if the dog moves around or scratches. Many eggs will fall off in the dog's favorite area or an area in which he spends a lot of time, such as his bed.

Once the eggs fall from the dog onto the carpet or furniture, they will hatch into larvae. This takes from one to ten days. Larvae are not particularly mobile and will usually travel only a few inches from where they hatch. However, they do have a tendency to move away from bright light and heavy traffic—under furniture and behind doors are common places to find high quantities of flea larvae.

The flea larvae feed on dead organic matter, including adult flea feces, until they are ready to change into adult fleas. Fleas will usually remain as larvae for around seven days. After this period, the larvae will pupate into protective pupae. While inside the pupae, the larvae will undergo metamorphosis and change into

EN GARDE: CATCHING FLEAS OFF GUARD!
Consider the following ways to arm yourself against fleas:

- Add a small amount of pennyroyal or eucalyptus oil to your dog's bath. These natural remedies repel fleas.
- Supplement your dog's food with fresh garlic (minced or grated) and a hearty amount of brewer's yeast, both of which ward off fleas.
- Use a flea comb on your dog daily. Submerge fleas in a cup of bleach to kill them quickly.
- Confine the dog to only a few rooms to limit the spread of fleas in the home.
- Vacuum daily...and get all of the crevices! Dispose of the bag every few days until the problem is under control.
- Wash your dog's bedding daily. Cover cushions where your dog sleeps with towels, and wash the towels often.

adult fleas. This can take as little time as a few days, but the adult fleas can remain inside the pupae waiting to hatch for up to two years. The pupae are signaled to hatch by certain stimuli, such as physical pressure—the pupae's being stepped on, heat from an animal's lying on the pupae or increased carbon-dioxide levels and vibrations—indicating that a suitable host is available.

Once hatched, the adult flea must feed within a few days. Once the adult flea finds a host, it will not leave voluntarily. It only becomes dislodged by grooming or the host animal's scratching. The adult flea will remain on the

PHOTO BY DWIGHT R. KUHN

host for the duration of its life unless forcibly removed.

TREATING THE ENVIRONMENT AND THE DOG

Treating fleas should be a two-pronged attack. First, the environment needs to be treated; this includes carpets and furniture, especially the dog's bedding and areas underneath furniture. The environment should be treated with a household spray containing an Insect Growth Regulator (IGR) and an insecticide to kill the adult fleas. Most IGRs are effective against eggs and larvae; they actually mimic the fleas' own hormones and stop the eggs and larvae from developing into adult fleas. There are currently no treatments available to attack the pupa stage of the life cycle, so the adult insecticide is used to kill the newly hatched adult fleas before they find a host. Most IGRs are active for many months, while adult insecticides are only active

A scanning electron micrograph of a dog or cat flea, *Ctenocephalides*, magnified more than 100x. This image has been colorized for effect.

S. E. M. BY DR DENNIS KUNKEL, UNIVERSITY OF HAWAII

THE LIFE CYCLE OF THE FLEA

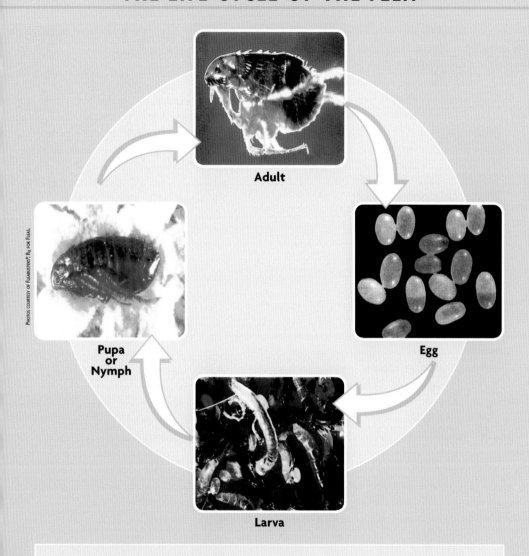

Adult

Egg

Larva

Pupa
or
Nymph

Fleas have been around for millions of years and have adapted to changing host animals. They are able to go through a complete life cycle in less than one month or they can extend their lives to almost two years by remaining as pupae or cocoons. They do not need blood or any other food for up to 20 months.

INSECT GROWTH REGULATOR (IGR)

Two types of products should be used when treating fleas—a product to treat the pet and a product to treat the home. Adult fleas represent less than 1% of the flea population. The pre-adult fleas (eggs, larvae and pupae) represent more than 99% of the flea population and are found in the environment; it is in the case of pre-adult fleas that products containing an Insect Growth Regulator (IGR) should be used in the home.

IGRs are a new class of compounds used to prevent the development of insects. They do not kill the insect outright, but instead use the insect's biology against it to stop it from completing its growth. Products that contain methoprene are the world's first and leading IGRs. Used to control fleas and other insects, this type of IGR will stop flea larvae from developing and protect the house for up to seven months.

for a few days.

When treating with a household spray, it is a good idea to vacuum before applying the product. This stimulates as many pupae as possible to hatch into adult fleas. The vacuum cleaner should also be treated with an insecticide to prevent the eggs and larvae that have been collected in the vacuum bag from hatching.

The second stage of treatment is to apply an adult insecticide to the dog. Traditionally, this would be in the form of a collar or a spray, but more recent innovations include digestible insecticides that poison the fleas when they ingest the dog's blood. Alternatively, there are drops that, when placed on the back of the dog's neck, spread throughout the hair and skin to kill adult fleas.

TICKS

Though not as common as fleas, ticks are found all over the tropical and temperate world. They don't bite, like fleas; they harpoon. They dig their sharp proboscis (nose) into the dog's skin and drink the blood. Their only food and drink is dog's

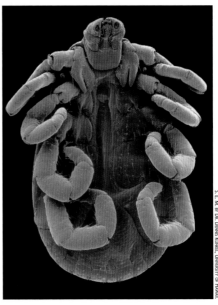

S.E.M. BY DR. DENNIS KUNKEL, UNIVERSITY OF HAWAII

blood. Dogs can get Lyme disease, Rocky Mountain spotted fever, tick bite paralysis and many other diseases from ticks. They may live where fleas are found and they like to hide in cracks or seams in walls. They are controlled the same way fleas are controlled.

The American dog tick, *Dermacentor variabilis*, may well be the most common dog tick in many geographical areas, especially those areas where the climate is hot and humid. Most dog ticks have life expectancies of a week to six months, depending upon climatic conditions. They can neither jump nor fly, but they can crawl slowly and can range up to 16 feet to reach a sleeping or unsuspecting dog.

MITES

Just as fleas and ticks can be problematic for your dog, mites can also lead to an itchy nuisance. Microscopic in size, mites are related to ticks and generally take up permanent residence on their host animal—in this case, your dog! The term *mange* refers to any infestation caused by one of the mighty mites, of which there are six varieties that concern dog owners.

Demodex mites cause a condition known as demodicosis (sometimes called red mange or

DEER-TICK CROSSING

The great outdoors may be fun for your dog, but it also is a home to dangerous ticks. Deer ticks carry a bacterium known as *Borrelia burgdorferi* and are most active in the autumn and spring. When infections are caught early, penicillin and tetracycline are effective antibiotics, but, if left untreated, the bacteria may cause neurological, kidney and cardiac problems as well as long-term trouble with walking and painful joints.

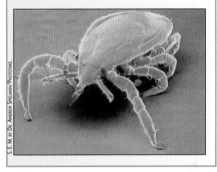

S.E.M. BY DR. ANDREW SPIELMAN/PHOTOTAKE.

PHOTO BY DR. DENNIS KUNKEL, UNIVERSITY OF HAWAII.

The head of an American dog tick, *Dermacentor variabilis*, enlarged and colorized for effect.

The mange mite, *Psoroptes bovis*, can infest cattle and other domestic animals.

Photo by James Hayden/Yoav/Phototake.

follicular mange), in which the mites live in the dog's hair follicles and sebaceous glands in larger-than-normal numbers. This type of mange is commonly passed from the dam to her puppies and usually shows up on the puppies' muzzles, though demodicosis is not transferable from one normal dog to another. Most dogs recover from this type of mange without any treatment, though topical therapies are commonly prescribed by the vet.

Human lice look like dog lice; the two are closely related.

Photo by Dwight R. Kuhn.

The *Cheyletiellosis* mite is the hook-mouthed culprit associated with "walking dandruff," a condition that affects dogs as well as cats and rabbits. This mite lives on the surface of the animal's skin and is readily transferable through direct or indirect contact with an affected animal. The dandruff is present in the form of scaly skin, which may or may not be itchy. If not treated, this mange can affect a whole kennel of dogs and can be spread to humans as well.

The *Sarcoptes* mite causes intense itching on the dog in the form of a condition known as scabies or sarcoptic mange. The cycle of the *Sarcoptes* mite lasts about three weeks, and the mites live in the top layer of the dog's skin (epidermis), preferably in areas with little hair. Scabies is highly contagious and can be passed to humans. Sometimes an allergic reaction to the mite worsens the severe itching associated with sarcoptic mange.

Ear mites, *Otodectes cynotis,* lead to otodectic mange, which most commonly affects the outer ear canal of the dog, though other areas can be affected as well. Dogs with ear-mite infestation commonly scratch at their ears, causing further irritation, and shake their heads. Dark brown droppings in the outer ear confirm the diagnosis. Your vet can prescribe a treatment to flush out the ears and kill any eggs in the ears. A complete month of treatment is necessary to cure the mange.

Two other mites, less common in dogs, include *Dermanyssus gallinae* (the poultry or red mite) and *Eutrombicula alfreddugesi* (the North American mite associated with trombiculidiasis or chigger infestation). The poultry mite frequently lives on chickens, but can transfer to dogs who spend time near farm animals. Chigger infestation affects dogs in the

---

NOT A DROP TO DRINK

Never allow your dog to swim in polluted water or public areas where water quality can be suspect. Even perfectly clear water can harbor parasites, many of which can cause serious to fatal illnesses in canines. Areas inhabited by waterfowl and other wildlife are especially dangerous.

---

central US who have exposure to woodlands. The types of mange caused by both of these mites are treatable by vets.

INTERNAL PARASITES

Most animals—fishes, birds and mammals, including dogs and humans—have worms and other parasites that live inside their bodies. According to Dr. Herbert R. Axelrod, the fish pathologist, there are two kinds of parasites: dumb and smart. The smart parasites live in peaceful cooperation with their hosts (symbiosis), while the dumb parasites kill their hosts. Most worm infections are relatively easy to control. If they are not controlled, they weaken the host dog to the point that other medical problems occur, but they do not kill the host as dumb parasites would.

A brown dog tick, *Rhipicephalus sanguineus*, is an uncommon but annoying tick found on dogs.
PHOTO BY CAROLINA BIOLOGICAL SUPPLY/PHOTOTAKE.

DO NOT MIX

Never mix parasite-control products without first consulting your vet. Some products can become toxic when combined with others and can cause fatal consequences.

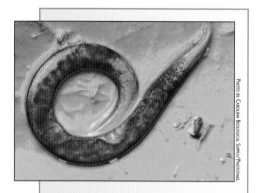

The roundworm *Rhabditis* can infect both dogs and humans.

The roundworm, *Ascaris lumbricoides.*

ROUNDWORMS

Average-size dogs can pass 1,360,000 roundworm eggs every day. For example, if there were only 1 million dogs in the world, the world would be saturated with thousands of tons of dog feces. These feces would contain around 15,000,000,000 roundworm eggs.

Up to 31% of home yards and children's sand boxes in the US contain roundworm eggs.

Flushing dog's feces down the toilet is not a safe practice because the usual sewage treatments do not destroy roundworm eggs.

Infected puppies start shedding roundworm eggs at three weeks of age. They can be infected by their mother's milk.

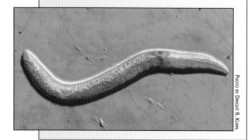

ROUNDWORMS

The roundworms that infect dogs are known scientifically as *Toxocara canis*. They live in the dog's intestines and shed eggs continually. It has been estimated that a dog produces about 6 or more ounces of feces every day. Each ounce of feces averages hundreds of thousands of roundworm eggs. There are no known areas in which dogs roam that do not contain roundworm eggs. The greatest danger of roundworms is that they infect people, too! It is wise to have your dog tested regularly for roundworms.

In young puppies, roundworms cause bloated bellies, diarrhea, coughing and vomiting, and are transmitted from the dam (through blood or milk). Affected puppies will not appear as animated as normal puppies. The worms appear spaghetti-like, measuring as long as 6 inches. Adult dogs can acquire roundworms through coprophagia (eating contaminated feces) or by killing rodents that carry roundworms.

Roundworm infection can kill puppies and cause severe problems in adults, as the hatched larvae travel to the lungs and trachea through the bloodstream. Cleanliness is the best preventative for roundworms. Always pick up after your dog and dispose of feces in appropriate receptacles.

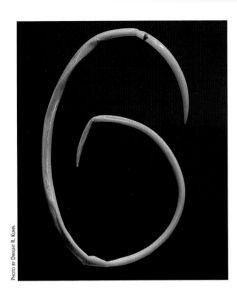

PHOTO BY DWIGHT R. KUHN.

HOOKWORMS

In the United States, dog owners have to be concerned about four different species of hookworm, the most common and most serious of which is *Ancylostoma caninum*, which prefers warm climates. The others are *Ancylostoma braziliense, Ancylostoma tubaeforme* and *Uncinaria stenocephala,* the latter of which is a concern to dogs living in the northern US and Canada, as this species prefers cold climates.

Hookworms are dangerous to humans as well as to dogs and cats, and can be the cause of severe anemia due to iron deficiency. The worm uses its teeth to attach itself to the dog's intestines and changes the site of its attachment about six times per day. Each time the worm reposi-

tions itself, the dog loses blood and can become anemic. *Ancylostoma caninum* is the most likely of the four species to cause anemia in the dog.

Symptoms of hookworm infection include dark stools, weight loss, general weakness, pale coloration and anemia, as well as possible skin problems. Fortunately, hookworms are easily purged from the affected dog with a number of medications that have proven effective. Discuss these with your vet. Most heartworm preventatives include a hookworm insecticide as well.

Owners also must be aware that hookworms can infect humans, who can acquire the larvae through exposure to contaminated feces. Since the worms cannot complete their life cycle on a human, the worms simply infest the skin and cause irritation. This condition is known as cutaneous larva migrans syndrome. As a preventative, use disposable gloves or a "poop-scoop" to pick up your dog's droppings and prevent your dog (or neighborhood cats) from defecating in children's play areas.

The hookworm, *Ancylostoma caninum.*

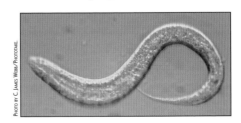

PHOTO BY C. JAMES WEBB/PHOTOTAKE.

The infective stage of the hookworm larva.

TAPEWORMS

Humans, rats, squirrels, foxes, coyotes, wolves and domestic dogs are all susceptible to tapeworm infection. Except in humans, tapeworms are usually not a fatal infection. Infected individuals can harbor 1000 parasitic worms.

Tapeworms, like some other types of worm, are hermaphroditic, meaning male and female in the same worm.

If dogs eat infected rats or mice, or anything else infected with tapeworm, they get the tapeworm disease. One month after attaching to a dog's intestine, the worm starts shedding eggs. These eggs are infective immediately. Infective eggs can live for a few months without a host animal.

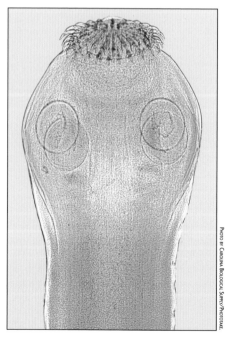

The head and rostellum (the round prominence on the scolex) of a tapeworm, which infects dogs and humans.

TAPEWORMS

There are many species of tapeworm, all of which are carried by fleas! The most common tapeworm affecting dogs is known as *Dipylidium caninum*. The dog eats the flea and starts the tapeworm cycle. Humans can also be infected with tapeworms—so don't eat fleas! Fleas are so small that your dog could pass them onto your hands, your plate or your food and thus make it possible for you to ingest a flea that is carrying tapeworm eggs.

While tapeworm infection is not life-threatening in dogs (smart parasite!), it can be the cause of a very serious liver disease for humans. About 50% of the humans infected with *Echinococcus multilocularis*, a type of tapeworm that causes alveolar hydatid, perish.

WHIPWORMS

In North America, whipworms are counted among the most common parasitic worms in dogs. The whipworm's scientific name is *Trichuris vulpis*. These worms attach themselves in the lower parts of the intestine, where they feed. Affected dogs may only experience upset tummies, colic and diarrhea. These worms, however, can live for months or years in the dog, beginning their larval stage in the small intestine, spending their adult stage in the large intestine and finally passing infective eggs through the dog's feces. The only way to detect whipworms is through a fecal examination, though this is not always foolproof. Treatment for whipworms is tricky, due to the worms' unusual life-cycle pattern, and very often dogs are reinfected due to exposure to infective eggs on the ground. The whipworm eggs can survive in the environment for as long as five years; thus, cleaning up droppings in your own backyard as well as in public places is absolutely essential for sanitation purposes and the health of your dog and others.

THREADWORMS
Though less common than roundworms, hookworms and those previously mentioned, threadworms concern dog owners in the southwestern US and Gulf Coast area where the climate is hot and humid. Living in the small intestine of the dog, this worm measures a mere 2 millimeters and is round in shape. Like that of the whipworm, the threadworm's life cycle is very complex and the eggs and larvae are passed through the feces. A deadly disease in humans, *Strongyloides* readily infects people, and the handling of feces is the most common means of transmission. Threadworms are most often seen in young puppies; bloody diarrhea and pneumonia are symptoms. Sick puppies must be isolated and treated immediately; vets recommend a follow-up treatment one month later.

HEARTWORM PREVENTATIVES

There are many heartworm preventatives on the market, many of which are sold at your veterinarian's office. These products can be given daily or monthly, depending on the manufacturer's instructions. All of these preventatives contain chemical insecticides directed at killing heartworms, which leads to some controversy among dog owners. In effect, heartworm preventatives are necessary evils, though you should determine how necessary based on your pet's lifestyle. There is no doubt that heartworm is a dreadful disease that threatens the lives of dogs. However, the likelihood of your dog's being bitten by an infected mosquito is slim in most places, and a mosquito-repellent (or an herbal remedy such as Wormwood or Black Walnut) is much safer for your dog and will not compromise his immune system (the way heartworm preventatives will). Should you decide to use the traditional preventative "medications," you can consider giving the pill every other or third month. Since the toxins in the pill will kill the heartworms at all stages of development, the pill would be effective in killing larvae, nymphs or adults, and it takes four months for the larvae to reach the adult stage. Thus, there is no rationale to poisoning the dog's system on a monthly basis. Lastly, do not give the pill during the winter months since there are no mosquitoes around to pass on their infection, unless you live in a tropical environment.

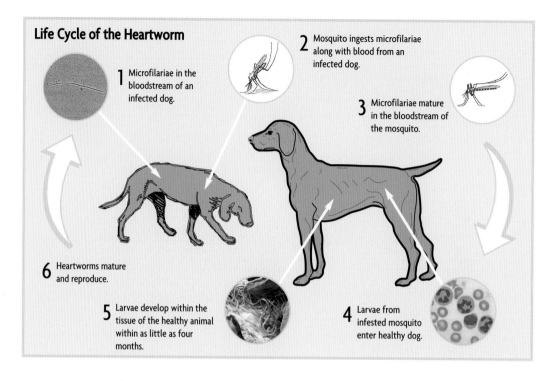

Life Cycle of the Heartworm

1 Microfilariae in the bloodstream of an infected dog.

2 Mosquito ingests microfilariae along with blood from an infected dog.

3 Microfilariae mature in the bloodstream of the mosquito.

6 Heartworms mature and reproduce.

5 Larvae develop within the tissue of the healthy animal within as little as four months.

4 Larvae from infested mosquito enter healthy dog.

HEARTWORMS

Heartworms are thin, extended worms up to 12 inches long, which live in a dog's heart and the major blood vessels surrounding it. Dogs may have up to 200 worms. Symptoms may be loss of energy, loss of appetite, coughing, the development of a pot belly and anemia.

Heartworms are transmitted by mosquitoes. The mosquito drinks the blood of an infected dog and takes in larvae with the blood. The larvae, called microfilariae, develop within the body of the mosquito and are passed on to the next dog bitten after the larvae mature. It takes two to three weeks for the larvae to develop to the infective stage within the body of the mosquito. Dogs are usually treated at about six weeks of age and maintained on a prophylactic dose given monthly.

Blood testing for heartworms is not necessarily indicative of how seriously your dog is infected. Although this is a dangerous disease, it is not easy for a dog to be infected. Discuss the various preventatives with your vet, as there are many different types now available. Together you can decide on a safe course of prevention for your dog.

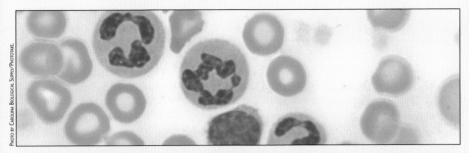

Magnified heartworm larvae, *Dirofilaria immitis*.

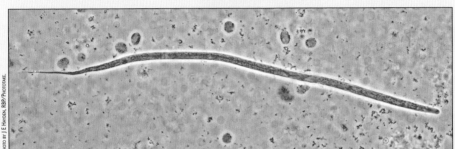

Heartworm, *Dirofilaria immitis*.

The heart of a dog infected with canine heartworm, *Dirofilaria immitis*.

HOMEOPATHY:

an alternative to conventional medicine

"Less is Most"

Using this principle, the strength of a homeopathic remedy is measured by the number of serial dilutions that were undertaken to create it. The greater the number of serial dilutions, the greater the strength of the homeopathic remedy. The potency of a remedy that has been made by making a dilution of 1 part in 100 parts (or 1/100) is 1c or 1cH. If this remedy is subjected to a series of further dilutions, each one being 1/100, a more dilute and stronger remedy is produced. If the remedy is diluted in this way six times, it is called 6c or 6cH. A dilution of 6c is 1 part in 1,000,000,000,000. In general, higher potencies in more frequent doses are better for acute symptoms and lower potencies in more infrequent doses are more useful for chronic, long-standing problems.

CURING OUR DOGS NATURALLY

Holistic medicine means treating the whole animal as a unique, perfect, living being. Generally, holistic treatments do not suppress the symptoms that the body naturally produces, as do most medications prescribed by conventional doctors and vets. Holistic methods seek to cure disease by regaining balance and harmony in the patient's environment. Some of these methods include use of nutritional therapy, herbs, flower essences, aromatherapy, acupuncture, massage, chiropractic and, of course, the most popular holistic approach, homeopathy.

Homeopathy is a theory or system of treating illness with small doses of substances which, if administered in larger quantities, would produce the symptoms that the patient already has. This approach is often described as "like cures like." Although modern veterinary medicine is geared toward the "quick fix," homeopathy relies on the belief that, given the time, the body is able to heal itself and return to its natural, healthy state.

Choosing a remedy to cure a problem in our dogs is the difficult part of homeopathy. Consult with your vet for a professional diagnosis of your dog's symptoms. Often these symptoms require immediate conventional care. If your vet is willing and knowledgeable, you may attempt a homeopathic remedy. Be aware that cortisone prevents homeopathic remedies from working. There are hundreds of possibilities and combinations to cure many problems in dogs, from basic physical problems such as excessive shedding, fleas or other parasites, unattractive doggy odor, bad breath, upset tummy, obesity,

dry, oily or dull coat, diarrhea, ear problems or eye discharge (including tears and dry or mucousy matter), to behavioral abnormalities such as fear of loud noises, habitual licking, poor appetite, excessive barking and various phobias. From alumina to zincum metallicum, the remedies span the planet and the imagination…from flowers and weeds to chemicals, insect droppings, diesel smoke and volcanic ash.

Using "Like to Treat Like"

Unlike conventional medicines that suppress symptoms, homeopathic remedies treat illnesses with small doses of substances that, if administered in larger quantities, would produce the symptoms that the patient already has. While the same homeopathic remedy can be used to treat different symptoms in different dogs, here are some interesting remedies and their uses.

Apis Mellifica
(made from honey bee venom) can be used for allergies or to reduce swelling that occurs in acutely infected kidneys.

Diesel Smoke
can be used to help control travel sickness.

Calcarea Fluorica
(made from calcium fluoride, which helps harden bone structure) can be useful in treating hard lumps in tissues.

Natrum Muriaticum
(made from common salt, sodium chloride) is useful in treating thin, thirsty dogs.

Nitricum Acidum
(made from nitric acid) is used for symptoms you would expect to see from contact with acids, such as lesions, especially where the skin joins the linings of body orifices or openings such as the lips and nostrils.

Symphytum
(made from the herb Knitbone, *Symphytum officianale*) is used to encourage bones to heal.

Urtica Urens
(made from the common stinging nettle) is used in treating painful, irritating rashes.

First Aid at a Glance

Burns
Place the affected area under cool water; use ice if only a small area is burnt.

Bee stings/Insect bites
Apply ice to relieve swelling; antihistamine dosed properly.

Animal bites
Clean any bleeding area; apply pressure until bleeding subsides; go to the vet.

Spider bites
Use cold compress and a pressurized pack to inhibit venom's spreading.

Antifreeze poisoning
Induce vomiting with hydrogen peroxide. Seek *immediate* veterinary help!

Fish hooks
Removal best handled by vet; hook must be cut in order to remove.

Snake bites
Pack ice around bite; contact vet quickly; identify snake for proper antivenin.

Car accident
Move dog from roadway with blanket; seek veterinary aid.

Shock
Calm the dog; keep him warm; seek immediate veterinary help.

Nosebleed
Apply cold compress to the nose; apply pressure to any visible abrasion.

Bleeding
Apply pressure above the area; treat wound by applying a cotton pack.

Heat stroke
Submerge dog in cold bath; cool down with fresh air and water; go to the vet.

Frostbite/Hypothermia
Warm the dog with a warm bath, electric blankets or hot water bottles.

Abrasions
Clean the wound and wash out thoroughly with fresh water; apply antiseptic.

 Remember: an injured dog may attempt to bite a helping hand from fear and confusion. Always muzzle the dog before trying to offer assistance.

Recognizing a Sick Dog

Unlike colicky babies and cranky children, our canine kids cannot tell us when they are feeling ill. Therefore, there are a number of signs that owners can identify to know that their dogs are not feeling well.

Take note for physical manifestations such as:

- unusual, bad odor, including bad breath
- excessive shedding
- wax in the ears, chronic ear irritation
- oily, flaky, dull haircoat
- mucus, tearing or similar discharge in the eyes
- fleas or mites
- mucus in stool, diarrhea
- sensitivity to petting or handling
- licking at paws, scratching face, etc.

Keep an eye out for behavioral changes as well including:

- lethargy, idleness
- lack of patience or general irritability
- lack of interest in food
- phobias (fear of people, loud noises, etc.)
- strange behavior, suspicion, fear
- coprophagia
- more frequent barking
- whimpering, crying

Get Well Soon

You don't need a DVM to provide good TLC to your sick or recovering dog, but you do need to pay attention to some details that normally wouldn't bother him. The following tips will aid Fido's recovery and get him back on his paws again:

- Keep his space free of irritating smells, like heavy perfumes and air fresheners.
- Rest is the best medicine! Avoid harsh lighting that will prevent your dog from sleeping. Shade him from bright sunlight during the day and dim the lights in the evening.
- Keep the noise level down. Animals are more sensitive to sound when they are sick.

- Be attentive to any necessary temperature adjustments. A dog with a fever needs a cool room and cold liquids. A bitch that is whelping or recovering from surgery will be more comfortable in a warm room, consuming warm liquids and food.
- You wouldn't send a sick child back to school early, so don't rush your dog back into a full routine until he seems absolutely ready.

Number-One Killer Disease in Dogs: CANCER

In every age, there is a word associated with a disease or plague that causes humans to shudder. In the 21st century, that word is "cancer." Just as cancer is the leading cause of death in humans, it claims nearly half the lives of dogs that die from a natural disease as well as half the dogs that die over the age of ten years.

Described as a genetic disease, cancer becomes a greater risk as the dog ages. Vets and dog owners have become increasingly aware of the threat of cancer to dogs. Statistics reveal that one dog in every five will develop cancer, the most common of which is skin cancer. Many cancers, including prostate, ovarian and breast cancer, can be avoided by spaying and neutering our dogs by the age of six months.

Early detection of cancer can save or extend a dog's life, so it is absolutely vital for owners to have their dogs examined by a qualified vet or oncologist immediately upon detection of any abnormality. Certain dietary guidelines have also proven to reduce the onset and spread of cancer. Foods based on fish rather than beef, due to the presence of Omega-3 fatty acids, are recommended. Other amino acids such as glutamine have significant benefits for canines, particularly those breeds that show a greater susceptibility to cancer.

Cancer management and treatments promise hope for future generations of canines. Since the disease is genetic, breeders should never breed a dog whose parents, grandparents and any related siblings have developed cancer. It is difficult to know whether to exclude an otherwise healthy dog from a breeding program, as the disease does not manifest itself until the dog's senior years.

RECOGNIZE CANCER WARNING SIGNS

Since early detection can possibly rescue your dog from becoming a cancer statistic, it is essential for owners to recognize the possible signs and seek the assistance of a qualified professional.

- Abnormal bumps or lumps that continue to grow
- Bleeding or discharge from any body cavity
- Persistent stiffness or lameness
- Recurrent sores or sores that do not heal
- Inappetence
- Breathing difficulties
- Weight loss
- Bad breath or odors
- General malaise and fatigue
- Eating and swallowing problems
- Difficulty urinating and defecating

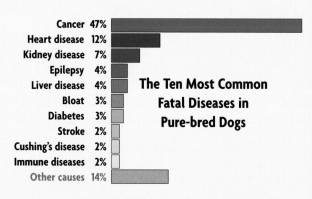

Disease	Percentage
Cancer	47%
Heart disease	12%
Kidney disease	7%
Epilepsy	4%
Liver disease	4%
Bloat	3%
Diabetes	3%
Stroke	2%
Cushing's disease	2%
Immune diseases	2%
Other causes	14%

The Ten Most Common Fatal Diseases in Pure-bred Dogs

CDS: COGNITIVE DYSFUNCTION SYNDROME
"Old-Dog Syndrome"

There are many ways for you to evaluate old-dog syndrome. Veterinarians have defined CDS (cognitive dysfunction syndrome) as the gradual deterioration of cognitive abilities. These are indicated by changes in the dog's behavior. When a dog changes his routine response, and maladies have been eliminated as the cause of these behavioral changes, then CDS is the usual diagnosis.

More than half the dogs over eight years old suffer from some form of CDS. The older the dog, the more chance he has of suffering from CDS. In humans, doctors often dismiss the CDS behavioral changes as part of "winding down."

There are four major signs of CDS: frequent potty accidents inside the home, sleeping much more or much less than normal, acting confused and failing to respond to social stimuli.

SYMPTOMS OF CDS

FREQUENT POTTY ACCIDENTS
- *Urinates in the house.*
- *Defecates in the house.*
- *Doesn't signal that he wants to go out.*

SLEEP PATTERNS
- *Awakens more slowly.*
- *Sleeps more than normal during the day.*
- *Sleeps less during the night.*

CONFUSION
- *Goes outside and just stands there.*
- *Appears confused with a faraway look in his eyes.*
- *Hides more often.*
- *Doesn't recognize friends.*
- *Doesn't come when called.*
- *Walks around listlessly and without a destination.*

FAILURE TO RESPOND TO SOCIAL STIMULI
- *Comes to people less frequently, whether called or not.*
- *Doesn't tolerate petting for more than a short time.*
- *Doesn't come to the door when you return home.*

ENGLISH FOXHOUND

The term *old* is a qualitative term. For dogs, as well as their masters, old is relative. Certainly we can all distinguish between a puppy English Foxhound and an adult English Foxhound—there are the obvious physical traits, such as size, appearance and facial expressions, and personality traits as well. Puppies and young dogs like to play with children. Children's natural exuberance is a good match for the seemingly endless energy of young dogs. They like to run, jump, chase and retrieve. When dogs grow up and cease their interaction with children, they are often thought of as being too old to play with the kids. On the other hand, if an English Foxhound is only exposed to people with quieter lifestyles, the dog's life will normally be less active and the decrease in his activity level as he ages will not be as obvious.

If people live to be 100 years old, dogs live to be 20 years old. While this may sound like a good rule of thumb, it is very inaccurate. When trying to compare dog years to human years, you cannot make a generalization about all dogs. You can make the generalization that about 12 years is the average lifespan for an English Foxhound, but life expectancies vary greatly from breed to breed.

Dogs in general are typically considered mature within three years, but they can reproduce even earlier. So it's more accurate to compare the first three years of a dog's life to seven times that of a comparable human. That means a 3-year-old dog is like a 21-year-old human. As the curve of comparison shows, however, there is no hard and fast rule for comparing dog and human ages. The comparison is made even more difficult, for not all humans age at the same rate.

GETTING OLD

The bottom line is simply that a dog is getting old when you think he is getting old because he slows down in his general activities, including walking, running, eating, jumping and retrieving. On the other hand, certain activities increase, like more sleeping, more barking and more repetition of habits like going to the door when you put your coat on without being called.

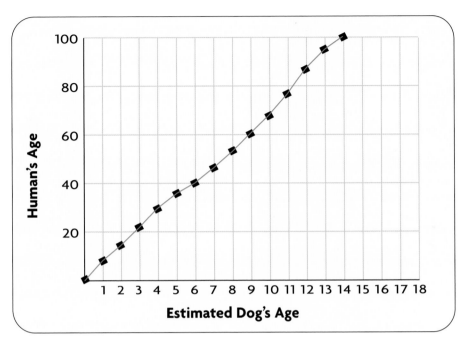

Estimated Dog's Age

WHAT TO LOOK FOR IN SENIORS

Most veterinarians and behaviorists use the seven-year mark as the time to consider a dog a "senior." This term does not imply that the dog is geriatric and has begun to fail in mind and body. Aging is essentially a slowing process. Humans readily admit that they feel a difference in their activity level from age 20 to 30, and then from 30 to 40, etc. By treating the seven-year-old dog as a senior, owners are able to implement certain therapeutic and preventative medical strategies with the help of their veterinarians.

A senior-care program should include at least two veterinary visits per year and screening sessions to determine the dog's health status, as well as nutritional counseling. Veterinarians determine the senior dog's health status through a blood smear for a complete blood count, serum chemistry profile with electrolytes, urinalysis, blood pressure check, electrocardiogram, ocular tonometry (pressure on the eyeball) and dental prophylaxis.

Such an extensive program for senior dogs is well advised before owners start to see the obvious physical signs of aging, such as slower and inhibited movement, graying, increased sleep/nap periods and disinterest in play and other activity. This

A little gray around the muzzle doesn't keep the English Foxhound from being a distinguished and alert companion in his senior years.

suffering from senility can become more impatient and irritable. Housesoiling accidents are associated with loss of mobility, kidney problems and loss of sphincter control as well as plaque accumulation, physiological brain changes and reactions to medications. Older dogs, just like young puppies, can suffer from separation anxiety, which can lead to excessive barking, whining, housesoiling and destructive behavior. Seniors may become fearful of everyday sounds, such as vacuum cleaners, heaters, thunder and passing traffic. Some dogs have difficulty sleeping, due to discomfort, the need for frequent potty visits and the like.

Owners should avoid spoiling the older dog with too many treats. Obesity is a common problem in older dogs and subtracts years from their lives.

preventative program promises a longer, healthier life for the aging dog. Among the physical problems common in aging dogs are the loss of sight and hearing, arthritis, kidney and liver failure, diabetes mellitus, heart disease and Cushing's disease (a hormonal disease).

In addition to the physical manifestations discussed, there are some behavioral changes and problems related to aging dogs. Dogs suffering from hearing or vision loss, dental discomfort or arthritis can become aggressive. Likewise, the near-deaf and/or blind dog may be startled more easily and react in an unexpectedly aggressive manner. Seniors

HORMONAL PROBLEMS

Although graying is normal and expected in older dogs, a flaky coat or loss of hair is not. Such coat problems may point to a hormonal problem. Hypothyroidism, in which the thyroid gland fails to produce the normal amount of hormones, is one such problem. Your veterinarian can treat hypothyroidism with an oral supplement. The condition is more common in certain breeds, so discuss its likelihood in your dog with your breeder and vet.

Keep the senior dog as trim as possible, since excess weight puts additional stress on the body's vital organs. Some breeders recommend supplementing the diet with foods high in fiber and lower in calories. Adding fresh vegetables and marrow broth to the senior's diet makes a tasty, low-calorie, low-fat supplement. Vets also offer specialty diets for senior dogs that are worth exploring.

Your dog, as he nears his twilight years, needs his owner's patience and good care more than ever. Never punish an older dog for an accident or abnormal behavior. For all the years of love, protection and companionship that your dog has provided, he deserves special attention and courtesies. The older dog may need to relieve himself at 3 a.m. because he can no longer hold it for eight hours. Older dogs may not be able to remain crated for more than two or three hours. It may be time to give up a sofa or chair to your old friend. Although he may not seem as enthusiastic about your attention and petting, he does appreciate the considerations you offer as he gets older.

Your English Foxhound does not understand why his world is slowing down. Owners must make their dogs' transition into the golden years as pleasant and rewarding as possible.

WHAT TO DO WHEN THE TIME COMES

You are never fully prepared to make a rational decision about putting your dog to sleep. It is very obvious that you love your English Foxhound or you would not be reading this book. Putting a loved dog to sleep is extremely difficult. It is a decision that must be made with your veterinarian. You are usually forced to make the decision when your dog experiences one or more life-threatening symptoms, requiring you to seek veterinary help. If the prognosis of the malady indicates the end is near and your beloved pet will only suffer more and experience no enjoyment for the balance of his life, then euthanasia is the right choice.

WHAT IS EUTHANASIA?

Euthanasia derives from the Greek, meaning *good death*. In other words, it means the planned, painless killing of a dog suffering from a painful, incurable

---

EUTHANASIA SERVICES
Euthanasia must be done by a licensed vet, who may be considerate enough to come to your home. There also may be societies for the prevention of cruelty to animals in your area. They often offer this service upon a vet's recommendation.

condition, or who is so aged that he cannot walk, see, eat or control his excretory functions.

Euthanasia is usually accomplished by injection with an overdose of an anesthesia or barbiturate. Aside from the prick of the needle, the experience is painless.

MAKING THE DECISION

The decision to euthanize your dog is never easy. The days during which the dog becomes ill and the end occurs can be unusually stressful for you. If this is your first experience with the death of a loved one, you may need the comfort dictated by your religious beliefs. If you are the head of the family and have children, you should have involved them in the decision of putting your English

> **TALK IT OUT**
> The more openly your family discusses the whole stressful occurrence of the aging and eventual loss of a beloved pet, the easier it will be for you when the time comes.

Foxhound to sleep. Usually your dog can be maintained on drugs for a few days at the vet's clinic in order to give you ample time to make a decision. During this time, talking with members of the family or religious representatives, or even people who have lived through this same experience, can ease the burden of your inevitable decision. In any case, euthanasia can be very stressful for the family of the dog.

Consult your vet to help you locate a pet cemetery in your area.

THE FINAL RESTING PLACE

Dogs can have some of the same privileges as humans. The remains of your beloved dog can be buried in a pet cemetery, which is generally expensive. If your dog has died at home, he can be buried in your yard in a place suitably marked with a special stone or a newly planted tree or bush. Alternatively, your dog can be cremated individually and the ashes returned to you. A less expensive option is mass cremation, although, of course, the ashes of individual dogs cannot then be returned.

Your vet can usually help you locate a pet cemetery or arrange cremation on your behalf if you choose one of these options. The cost of these options should always be discussed frankly and openly with your veterinarian.

Many pet cemeteries have facilities for displaying urns that store dogs' ashes.

GETTING ANOTHER DOG?

The grief of losing your beloved dog will be as lasting as the grief of losing a human friend or relative. In most cases, if your dog died of old age (if there is such a thing), he had slowed down considerably. Do you want a new English Foxhound puppy? Or are you better off finding a more mature English Foxhound, say two to three years of age, which will usually be house-trained and will have an already developed personality. In this case, you can find out if you like each other after a few hours of being together.

The decision is, of course, your own. Do you want another English Foxhound or perhaps a different breed so as to avoid comparison with your beloved friend? Most people usually stay with the same breed because they know (and love) the characteristics of that breed. Then, too, they often know people who have the same breed and perhaps they are lucky enough that a breeder whom they know and respect expects a litter soon. What could be better?

TO THE RESCUE

Some people choose to adopt or "rescue" an older dog instead of buying a new puppy. Some older dogs may have come from abusive environments and be fearful, while other dogs may have developed many bad habits; both situations can present challenges to their new owners. Training an older dog will take more time and patience, but persistence and an abundance of praise and love can transform a dog into a well-behaved, loyal companion.

SHOWING YOUR
ENGLISH FOXHOUND

When you purchase your English Foxhound, you will make it clear to the breeder whether you want one just as a lovable companion and pet, if you are seeking a future hunting dog or if you hope to be buying an English Foxhound with show prospects. No reputable breeder will sell you a young puppy and tell you that it is *definitely* of show quality, for so much can go wrong during the early months of a puppy's development. If you plan to show, what you will hopefully have acquired is a puppy with "show potential."

To the novice, exhibiting an English Foxhound in the show ring may look easy, but it takes a lot of hard work and devotion to do top winning at a show such as the prestigious Westminster Kennel Club dog show, not to mention a little luck, too!

The first concept that the canine novice learns when watching a dog show is that each dog first competes against members of his own breed. Once the judge has selected the best member of each breed (Best of Breed), provided that the show is judged on a Group system, that chosen dog will compete with other dogs in his group. Finally, the dogs chosen first in each group will compete for Best in Show.

The second concept that you must understand is that the dogs are not actually compared against one another. The judge compares each dog against his breed standard, the written description of the ideal specimen that is approved by the American Kennel Club (AKC). While some early breed standards were indeed based on specific dogs that were famous or popular, many dedicated enthusiasts say that a perfect specimen, as described in the standard, has never walked into a show ring, has never been bred and, to the woe of dog breeders around the globe, does not exist. Breeders attempt to get as close to this ideal as possible with every litter, but theoretically the "perfect" dog is so elusive that it is impossible. (And if the "perfect" dog were born, breeders and judges would never agree that it was indeed "perfect.")

If you are interested in

exploring the world of dog showing, your best bet is to join your local breed club or the national parent club, which is the English Foxhound Club of America. These clubs often host both regional and national specialties, shows only for English Foxhounds, which can include conformation as well as obedience trials and other performance events. Even if you have no intention of competing with your English Foxhound, a specialty is like a festival for lovers of the breed who congregate to share their favorite topic: Foxhounds! Clubs also send out newsletters, and some organize training days and seminars in order that people may learn more about their chosen breed. To locate the breed club closest to you, contact the American Kennel Club, which furnishes the rules and regulations for all of these events plus general dog registration and other basic requirements of dog ownership.

The American Kennel Club offers three kinds of conformation shows: An all-breed show (for all AKC-recognized breeds), a specialty show (for one breed only, usually sponsored by the parent club) and a Group show (for all breeds in the group). For a dog to become an AKC champion of record, the dog must accumulate 15 points at the shows from at least three

CLUB CONTACTS

You can get information about dog shows from the national kennel clubs:

American Kennel Club
5580 Centerview Dr., Raleigh, NC 27606-3390
www.akc.org

United Kennel Club
100 E. Kilgore Road, Kalamazoo, MI 49002
www.ukcdogs.com

Canadian Kennel Club
89 Skyway Ave., Suite 100, Etobicoke, Ontario
M9W 6R4 Canada
www.ckc.ca

The Kennel Club
1-5 Clarges St., Piccadilly, London
W1Y 8AB, UK
www.the-kennel-club.org.uk

MEET THE AKC

The American Kennel Club is the main governing body of the dog sport in the United States. Founded in 1884, the AKC consists of 500 or more independent dog clubs plus 4,500 affiliate clubs, all of which follow the AKC rules and regulations. Additionally, the AKC maintains a registry for pure-bred dogs in the US and works to preserve the integrity of the sport and its continuation in the country. Over 1,000,000 dogs are registered each year, representing about 150 recognized breeds. There are over 15,000 competitive events held annually for which over 2,000,000 dogs enter to participate. Dogs compete to earn over 40 different titles, from Champion to Companion Dog to Master Agility Champion.

---

different judges, including two "majors." A "major" is defined as a three-, four- or five-point win, and the number of points per win is determined by the number of dogs entered in the show on that day. Depending on the breed, the number of points that are awarded varies. More dogs are needed to rack up the points in the more popular breeds, and less dogs are needed in the less popular breeds. The English Foxhound's numbers are low in the US, so the breed has relatively small entries at all-breed shows.

At any dog show, only one dog and one bitch of each breed can win points. Dog showing does not offer "co-ed" classes. Dogs and bitches never compete against each other in the classes. Non-champion dogs are called "class dogs" because they compete in one of five classes. Dogs are entered in a particular class depending on age and previous show wins. To begin, there is the Puppy Class (for 6- to 9-month-olds and for 9- to 12-month-olds); this class is followed by the Novice Class (for dogs that have not won any first prizes except in the Puppy Class or three first prizes in the Novice Class and have not accumulated any points toward their championship); the Bred-by-Exhibitor Class (for dogs handled by their breeders or by one of the breeder's immediate family); the American-bred Class (for dogs bred in the US); and the Open Class (for any dog that is not a champion).

The judge at the show begins judging the Puppy Class, first dogs and then bitches, and proceeds through the classes. The judge places his winners first through fourth in each class. In the Winners Class, the first-place winners of each class compete with one another to determine Winners Dog and Winners Bitch. The judge also places a Reserve Winners Dog and Reserve Winners Bitch, which could be awarded the points in the case of a disqualification. The Winners Dog and Winners Bitch, the two that are awarded the points for the breed, then compete with any champions of record (often called "specials") entered in the show. The judge reviews the Winners Dog, Winners Bitch and all of the champions to select his Best of Breed. The Best of Winners is selected between the Winners Dog and Winners Bitch. Were one of these two to be selected Best of Breed, he or she would automatically be named Best of Winners as well. Finally the judge selects his Best of Opposite Sex to the Best of Breed winner.

At a Group show or all-breed show, the Best of Breed winners from each breed then compete against one another for Group One through Group Four. The judge compares each Best of Breed to the breed standard, and the dog that most closely lives up to the ideal for his breed is selected as Group One. Finally, all seven group winners (from the Hound Group, Sporting Group, Toy Group, etc.) compete for Best in Show.

To find out about dog shows in your area, you can subscribe to the American Kennel Club's monthly magazine, the *American Kennel Gazette* and the accompanying *Events Calendar*. You can also look in your local newspaper for advertisements for dog shows in your area or go on the Internet to the AKC's website, www.akc.org.

If your English Foxhound is six months of age or older and registered with the AKC, you can enter him in a dog show where the breed is offered classes. Provided that your English Foxhound does not have a disqualifying fault, he can compete. Only unaltered dogs can be entered in a dog show, so if you have spayed or neutered your English Foxhound, your dog cannot compete in conformation shows. The reason for this is simple. Dog shows are the main forum to prove which

PRACTICE AT HOME
If you have decided to show your dog, you must train him to gait around the ring by your side at the correct pace and pattern, and to tolerate being handled and examined by the judge. Most breeds require complete dentition, all breeds require a particular bite (scissors, level or undershot) and all males must have two apparently normal testicles fully descended into the scrotum. Enlist family and friends to hold mock trials in your yard to prepare your future champion!

representatives of a breed are worthy of being bred. Only dogs that have achieved championships—the AKC "seal of approval" for quality in pure-bred dogs—should be bred. Altered dogs, however, can participate in other AKC events such as obedience trials and the Canine Good Citizen® program.

Before you actually step into the ring, you would be well advised to sit back and observe the judge's ring procedure. If it is your first time in the ring, do not be over-anxious and run to the front of the line. Allow the steward to direct you and your dog to the proper place. The judge asks each handler to "stack" the dog, hopefully showing the dog off to his best advantage. The judge will observe the dog from a distance and from different angles, and approach the dog to check his teeth, overall structure, alertness and muscle tone, as well as consider how well the dog "conforms" to the standard. Most importantly, the judge will have the exhibitor move the dog around the ring in some pattern that he should specify (another advantage to not going first, but always listen since some judges change their directions—and the judge is always right!). Finally, the judge will give the dog one last look before moving on to the next exhibitor.

If you are not in the top four in your class at your first show, do not be discouraged. Be patient and consistent, and you may eventually find yourself in a winning line-up. Remember that the winners were once in your shoes and have devoted many hours and much money to earn the placement. If you find that your dog is losing every time and never getting a nod, it may be time to consider a different dog sport or to just enjoy your English Foxhound as a pet. Parent clubs offer other events, such as agility, field events, obedience, instinct tests and more, which may be of interest to the owner of a well-trained English Foxhound.

OBEDIENCE TRIALS
Obedience trials in the US trace back to the early 1930s when organized obedience events were developed to demonstrate how well dog and owner could work together. The pioneer of obedience trials is Mrs. Helen Whitehouse Walker, a Standard Poodle fancier, who designed a series of exercises after the Associated Sheep, Police, Army Dog Society of Great Britain. Since the days of Mrs. Walker, obedience trials have grown by leaps and bounds, and today there are over 2,000 trials held in the US every year, with more than 100,000 dogs competing.

Any AKC-registered dog can enter an obedience trial, regardless of conformational disqualifications or neutering.

Obedience trials are divided into three levels of progressive difficulty. At the first level, the Novice, dogs compete for the title Companion Dog (CD); at the intermediate level, the Open, dogs compete for the title Companion Dog Excellent (CDX); and at the advanced level, the Utility, dogs compete for the title Utility Dog (UD). Classes are sub-divided into "A" (for beginners) and "B" (for more experienced handlers). A perfect score at any level is 200, and a dog must score 170 or better to earn a "leg," of which three are needed to earn the title. To earn points, the dog must score more than 50% of the available points in each exercise; the possible points range from 20 to 40.

Each level consists of a different set of exercises. In the Novice level, the dog must heel on- and off-lead, come, long sit, long down and stand for examination. These skills are the basic ones required for a well-behaved "Companion Dog." The Open level requires that the dog perform the same exercises as in the Novice, but without a leash for extended lengths of time, as well as retrieve a dumbbell, broad jump and drop

on recall. In the Utility level, dogs must perform ten difficult exercises, including scent discrimination, hand signals for basic commands, directed jump and directed retrieve.

Once a dog has earned the UD title, he can compete with other proven obedience dogs for the coveted title of Utility Dog Excellent (UDX), which requires that the dog win "legs" in ten

Whether it's your first time in the ring or your 1000th, dress the part. Exhibitors should look as well put together as their dogs.

shows. Utility Dogs who earn "legs" in Open B and Utility B earn points toward their Obedience Trial Champion title. In 1977, the title Obedience Trial Champion (OTCh.) was established by the AKC. To become an OTCh., a dog needs to earn 100 points, which requires three first places in Open B and Utility under three different judges.

The Grand Prix of obedience trials, the AKC National Obedience Invitational gives qualifying Utility Dogs the chance to win the newest and highest title: National Obedience Champion (NOC). Only the top 25 ranked obedience dogs, plus any dog ranked in the top 3 in his breed, are allowed to compete.

AGILITY TRIALS

Having had its origins in the UK back in 1977, agility had its official AKC beginning in the US in August 1994, when the first licensed agility trials were held. The AKC allows all registered breeds (including Miscellaneous Class breeds) to participate, providing the dog is 12 months of age or older. Agility is designed so that the handler demonstrates how well the dog can work at his side. The handler directs his dog over an obstacle course that includes jumps as well as tires, the dog walk, weave poles, pipe tunnels, collapsed tunnels, etc. While working his way through the course, the dog must keep one eye and ear on the handler and the rest of his body on the course. The handler gives verbal and hand signals to guide the dog through the course.

The first organization to promote agility trials in the US was the United States Dog Agility Association, Inc. (USDAA), which was established in 1986 and spawned numerous member clubs around the country. Both the USDAA and the AKC offer titles to winning dogs. Three titles are available through the USDAA: Agility Dog (AD), Advanced Agility Dog (AAD) and Master Agility Dog (MAD). The AKC offers Novice Agility (NA), Open Agility (OA), Agility Excellent (AX) and Master Agility Excellent (MX). Beyond these four AKC titles,

TEMPERAMENT PLUS

Although it seems that physical conformation is the only factor considered in the show ring, temperament is also of utmost importance. An aggressive or fearful dog should not be shown, as bad behavior will not be tolerated and may pose a threat to the judge, other exhibitors, you and your dog.

FIELD TRIALS AND WORKING TESTS IN THE UK

In the English Foxhound's homeland, Britain, where hunting with hounds has a long and rich history, Foxhounds (as well as the Gundog breeds and the Working breeds) participate in working tests and field trials sanctioned by England's Kennel Club. Working tests are frequently used to prepare dogs for field trials, the purpose of which is to heighten the instincts and natural abilities of gundogs. Live game is not used in working tests. Unlike field trials, working tests do not count toward a dog's record at The Kennel Club, though the same judges often oversee working tests.

Field trials began in England in 1947 and are only moderately popular among dog folk. However, breeders of Working and Gundog breeds concern themselves with the field abilities of their dogs, and certain breeds must qualify in the field as well as in the show ring in order to become full champions. Upon gaining three Challenge Certificates in the show ring, the dog is designated a Show Champion (Sh. Ch.). The title Champion (Ch.) requires that the dog gain an award at a field trial, be a "special qualifier" at a field trial or pass a "special show dog qualifier" judged by a field-trial judge on a shooting day.

dogs can win additional ones in "jumper" classes, Jumpers with Weave Novice (NAJ), Open (OAJ) and Excellent (MXJ), which lead to the ultimate title(s): MACH, Master Agility Champion. Dogs can continue to add number designations to the MACH titles, indicating how many times the dog has met the MACH requirements, such as MACH1, MACH2 and so on.

Agility is great fun for dog and owner with many rewards for everyone involved. Interested owners should join a training club that has obstacles and experienced agility handlers who can introduce you and your dog to the "ropes" (and tires, tunnels, etc.).

TRACKING

Any dog is capable of tracking, using his nose to follow a trail. The English Foxhound is blessed with a very keen nose, and tracking tests are exciting and competitive ways to test your English Foxhound's natural scenting ability. The AKC started tracking tests in 1937, when the first AKC-licensed test took place as a part of the Utility level at an obedience trial. Ten years later in 1947, the AKC offered the first title, Tracking Dog (TD). It was not until 1980 that the AKC added the title Tracking Dog Excellent (TDX), which was followed by the title Versatile Surface Tracking (VST) in 1995. The title Champion Tracker (CT)

Foxhound clubs sponsor events that allow dogs to work in packs as they were bred to do.

breeds of the Sporting Group as well as the Beagles, Dachshunds and Bassets of the Hound Group, the English Foxhound (and other pack-hunting breeds such as the American Foxhound and Harrier), due to its pack-hunting nature, is not ideally suited to events designed for dogs that hunt one-on-one with their masters. The two major clubs in the US that organize and promote hunts and shows for the Foxhound breeds are the Foxhound Club of North America (www.fcna.org) and the Masters of Foxhounds Association of America (www.mfha.org). These clubs host performance trials and, under their auspices, regional clubs host hunts and hound shows.

is awarded to a dog who has earned all three titles.

In the beginning level of tracking, the owner follows the dog through a field on a long lead. To earn the TD title, the dog must follow a track laid by a human 30 to 120 minutes prior. The track is about 500 yards with up to 5 directional changes. The TDX requires that the dog follow a track that is 3 to 5 hours old over a course up to 1,000 yards with up to 7 directional changes. The VST requires that the dog follow a track up to 5 hours old through an urban setting.

HOUND SHOWS AND HUNTING EVENTS
While the AKC offers field trials and hunting events for the retrievers, pointers and spaniel

In a hound performance trial, for example, a pack hunt is organized, with various packs entered. During the course of the hunt, which is usually a two-day event, dogs are judged and scored individually in the areas of hunting, trailing, speed and drive and endurance. Areas of competition at hound shows include conformation classes and pack classes; in the latter, dogs are judged as a group, based on performance and uniformity. Interested owners should contact these clubs to find out how to register their dogs and become involved in these events.

ENGLISH FOXHOUND

As an English Foxhound owner, you have selected your dog so that you and your loved ones can have a companion, a weekend hunter, a friend and a four-legged family member. You invest time, money and effort to care for and train the family's new charge. Of course, this chosen canine behaves perfectly! Well, perfectly like a *dog*.

When discussing the English Foxhound, owners have much to consider. This is a very intelligent breed, and very pack-oriented, so these things pose challenges to those wishing to own an English Foxhound as a family pet. Add to this the dog's remarkable industry and high energy level, and owners must be ready to put their thinking caps on when dealing with the English Foxhound.

THINK LIKE A DOG

Dogs do not think like humans, nor do humans think like dogs, though we try. Unfortunately, a dog is incapable of figuring out how humans think, so the responsibility falls on the owner to adopt a viable canine mindset. Dogs cannot rationalize, and they exist in the present moment. Many a dog owner makes the mistake in training of thinking

that he can reprimand his dog for something the dog did a while ago. Basically, you cannot even reprimand a dog for something he did 20 seconds ago! Either catch him in the act or forget it! It is a waste of your and your dog's time—in his mind, you are reprimanding him for whatever he is doing at that moment.

The following behavioral problems represent some which owners most commonly encounter. Every dog is unique and every situation is unique. No author could purport for you to solve your English Foxhound's problem simply by reading a chapter in a breed book. Here we outline some basic "dogspeak" so that owners' chances of solving

Are you fluent in "dog"? In canine language, the male's lifting his leg means he is leaving a message for other dogs that pass by.

behavioral problems are increased. Discuss bad habits with your veterinarian and he can recommend a behavioral specialist to consult in appropriate cases when necessary. Since behavioral abnormalities are the leading reason for owners' abandoning their pets, we hope that you will make a valiant effort to solve your English Foxhound's problem. Patience and understanding are virtues that must dwell in every pet-loving household.

AGGRESSION

Aggression can be a problem in dogs of any breed, even in those breeds not known for aggressive behavior. Aggression, when not controlled, always becomes dangerous. An aggressive dog, no matter the size, may lunge at, bite or even attack a person or another dog. Aggressive behavior is not to be tolerated. It is more

than just inappropriate behavior; it is not safe. It is painful for a family to watch their dog become unpredictable in his behavior to the point where they are afraid of him. While not all aggressive behavior is dangerous, things like growling, baring teeth, etc., can be frightening. It is important to ascertain why the dog is acting in this manner. Aggression is a display of dominance, and the dog should not have the dominant role in his pack, which is, in this case, your family.

It is important not to challenge an aggressive dog, as this could provoke an attack. Observe your English Foxhound's body language. Does he make direct eye contact and stare? Does he try to make himself as large as possible: ears pricked, chest out, tail erect? Height and size signify authority in a dog pack—being taller or "above" another dog literally means that he is "above" in the social status. These body signals tell you that your English Foxhound thinks he is in charge, a problem that needs to be addressed. An aggressive dog is unpredictable: you never know when he is going to strike and what he is going to do. You cannot understand why a dog that is playful and loving one minute is growling and snapping the next.

Fear is a common cause of aggression in dogs. If you can

"Pleased to meet you"! After a brief getting-to-know-you period, Foxhounds become comfortable with other dogs quite easily.

isolate what brings out the fear reaction, you can help the dog get over it. Supervise your English Foxhound's interactions with people and other dogs, and praise the dog when it goes well. If he starts to act aggressively in a situation, correct him and remove him from the situation. Do not let people approach the dog and start petting him without your express permission. That way, you can have the dog sit to accept petting, and praise him when he behaves properly. You are focusing on praise and on modifying his behavior by rewarding him when he acts appropriately. By being gentle and by supervising his interactions, you are showing him that there is no need to be afraid or defensive.

The best solution is to consult a behavioral specialist, one who has experience with the English Foxhound or similar breeds if possible. Together, perhaps you can pinpoint the cause of your dog's aggression and do something about it. An aggressive dog cannot be trusted, and a dog that cannot be trusted is not safe to have as a family pet.

SEXUAL BEHAVIOR

Dogs exhibit certain sexual behaviors that may have influenced your choice of male or female when you first purchased

NO BUTTS ABOUT IT!
Dogs get to know each other by sniffing each other's backsides. It seems that each dog has a telltale odor, probably created by the anal glands. It also distinguishes sex and signals when a female will be receptive to a male's attention. Some dogs snap at another dog's intrusion of their private parts.

your English Foxhound. To some extent, spaying/neutering will eliminate these behaviors, but if you are purchasing a dog that you wish to show or breed, you should be aware of what you will have to deal with throughout the dog's life.

Female dogs usually have two estruses per year, with each season lasting about three weeks. These are the only times in which a female dog will mate, and she usually will not allow this until the second week of the cycle. If a bitch is not bred during the heat cycle, it is not uncommon for her to experience a false pregnancy, in which her mammary glands swell and she exhibits maternal tendencies toward toys or other objects.

With male dogs, owners must be aware that whole dogs (dogs who are not neutered) have the natural inclination to mark their territory. Males mark their territory by spraying small amounts of urine as they lift their legs in a macho ritual. Marking can occur both outdoors in the yard and around the neighborhood as well as indoors on furniture legs, curtains and the sofa. Such behavior can be very frustrating for the owner; early training is strongly urged before the "urge" strikes your dog. Neutering the male at an appropriate early age can solve this problem before it becomes a habit.

Other problems associated with males are wandering and mounting. Both of these habits, of course, belong to the unneutered dog, whose sexual drive leads him away from home in search of the bitch in heat. Males will mount females in heat, as well as any other dog, male or female, that happens to catch their fancy. Other possible mounting partners include his owner, the furniture, guests to the home and strangers on the street. Discourage such

behavior early on.

Owners must further recognize that mounting is not merely a sexual expression but also one of dominance, seen in males and females alike. Be consistent and persistent and you will find that you can "move mounters."

CHEWING

The national canine pastime is chewing! Every dog loves to sink his "canines" into a tasty bone, or whatever else is available. Dogs need to chew, to massage their gums, to make their new teeth feel better and to exercise their jaws. This is a natural behavior deeply imbedded in all things canine. Our role as owners is not to stop chewing, but to redirect it to positive, chew-worthy objects. Be an informed owner and purchase proper chew toys like strong nylon bones made for active dogs like your English Foxhound. Be sure that the devices are safe and durable, since your dog's safety is at risk. Again, the owner is responsible for ensuring a dog-proof environment.

The best answer is prevention: that is, put your shoes, handbags and other tasty objects in their proper places (out of the reach of the growing canine mouth). Direct your puppy to his toys whenever you see him tasting the furniture legs or your pant leg. Make a loud noise to attract the pup's attention, immediately escort him to his chew toy and engage him with the toy for at least four minutes, praising and encouraging him all the while.

Some trainers recommend deterrents, such as hot pepper or another bitter spice or a product designed for this purpose, to discourage the dog from chewing unwanted objects. This is sometimes reliable, though not as often as the manufacturers of such products claim. Test out these products with your own dog before investing in large quantities.

JUMPING UP

Jumping up is a dog's friendly way of saying hello! Some dog owners do not mind when their dog jumps up, but the problem arises when guests come to the house and the dog greets them in the same manner—whether they like it or not! However friendly the greeting may be, chances are your visitors will not appreciate being knocked over by your large and boisterous English Foxhound. The dog will not be able to distinguish upon whom he can jump and whom he cannot. Therefore, it is best to discourage this behavior entirely.

Pick a command such as "Off" (avoid using "Down" since you will use that for the dog to lie down) and tell him "Off" when

NO JUMPING

Stop a dog from jumping up before he jumps. If he is getting ready to jump onto you, simply walk away. If he jumps up on you before you can turn away, lift your knee so that it bumps him in the chest. Do not be forceful. Your dog soon will realize that jumping up is not a productive way of getting attention.

he jumps up. Place him on the ground on all fours and have him sit, praising him the whole time. Always lavish him with praise and petting when he is in the sit position. In this way, you can give him a warm affectionate greeting, let him know that you are as pleased to see him as he is to see you and instill good manners at the same time!

DIGGING

Digging, which is seen as a destructive behavior to humans, is actually quite a natural behavior in dogs. Although your English Foxhound is not one of the "earth dogs" (also known as terriers), any dog's desire to dig can be irrepressible and most frustrating to his owners. When digging occurs in your yard, it is actually a normal behavior redirected into something the dog can do in his everyday life. In the wild, a dog would be actively seeking food, making his own shelter, etc. He would be using his paws in a purposeful manner for his survival. Since you provide him with food and shelter, he has no need to use his paws for these purposes, and so the energy that he would be using manifests itself in the form of holes all over your yard and flowerbeds.

Perhaps your dog is digging as a reaction to boredom—it is somewhat similar to someone's eating a whole bag of chips in front of the TV—because they are there and there is not anything better to do! Basically, the answer is to provide the dog with adequate play and exercise so that his mind and paws are occupied, and so that he feels as if he is doing something useful.

Of course, digging is easiest to control if it is stopped as soon as possible, but it is often hard to catch a dog in the act, especially if he spends time alone in the yard. If your dog is a compulsive digger and is not easily distracted

by other activities, you can designate an area on your property where it is okay for him to dig. If you catch him digging in an off-limits area of the yard, immediately bring him to the approved area and praise him for digging there. Keep a close eye on him so that you can catch him in the act—that is the only way to make him understand what is permitted and what is not. If you bring him to a hole he dug an hour ago and tell him "No," he will understand that you are not fond of holes, dirt or flowers. If you catch him while he is stifle-deep in your tulips, that is when he will get your message.

BARKING
Dogs cannot talk—oh, what they would say if they could! Instead, barking is a dog's way of "talking." It can be somewhat frustrating because it is not always easy to tell what a dog means by his bark—is he excited, happy, frightened or angry? Whatever it is that the dog is trying to say, he should not be punished for barking. Only when the barking becomes excessive, and when the excessive barking becomes a bad habit, does the behavior need to be modified.

One of the English Foxhound's most prominent and most valued traits is his voice, so purposeful use of his bark should not be discouraged. If an intruder came into your home in the middle of the night and your English Foxhound barked a warning, wouldn't you be pleased? You would probably deem your dog a hero, a wonderful guardian and protector of the home. However, if a friend drops by unexpectedly, rings the doorbell and is greeted with a sudden sharp bark, you would probably be annoyed at the dog. But in reality, isn't this just the same behavior? The dog does not know any better...unless he sees who is at the door and it is someone he knows, he will bark as a means of vocalizing that his (and your) territory is being "threatened." While your friend is not posing a threat, it is all the same to the dog. Barking is his means of letting you know that there is an intrusion, whether friend or foe, on your property. This type of barking is instinctive and should not be discouraged.

Excessive habitual barking, however, is a problem that should be corrected early on. As your English Foxhound grows up, you will be able to tell when his barking is purposeful and when it is for no reason. You will become able to distinguish your dog's different barks and their meanings. For example, the bark when someone comes to the door will be different than the bark when he is excited to see you. It is similar to a person's tone of voice,

BARKING STANCE
Did you know that a dog is less likely to bark when sitting than standing? Watch your dog the next time that you suspect he is about to start barking. You'll notice that as he does, he gets up on all four feet. Hence, when teaching a dog to stop barking, it helps to get him to sit before you command him to be quiet.

except that the dog has to rely totally on tone of voice because he does not have the benefit of using words. An incessant barker will be evident at an early age.

There are some things that encourage a dog to bark. For example, if your dog barks non-stop for a few minutes and you give him a treat to quiet him, he believes that you are rewarding him for barking. He will associate barking with getting a treat, and will keep doing it until he is rewarded. On the other hand, if you give him a command such as "Quiet" and praise him after he has stopped barking for a few seconds, he will get the idea that being "quiet" is what you want him to do.

FOOD STEALING
Is your dog devising ways of stealing food from your coffee table or countertop? If so, you must answer the following questions: Is your English

Foxhound hungry, or is he "constantly famished" like every other chow hound? Why is there food out within the dog's reach? Face it, some dogs are more food-motivated than others. Some dogs are totally obsessed by food and can only think of their next meal. Food stealing is terrific fun and always yields a great reward—*food*, glorious food.

Your goal as an owner, therefore, is to be sensible about where food is placed in the home and to reprimand your dog whenever he is caught in the act of stealing. But remember, only reprimand your dog if you actually see him stealing, not later when the crime is discovered; that will be of no use at all and will only serve to confuse him.

BEGGING

Just like food stealing, begging is a favorite pastime of hungry puppies! It yields that same tasty reward—food! Dogs quickly learn that their owners keep the "good food" for ourselves, and that we humans do not dine on kibble

alone. Begging is a conditioned response related to a specific stimulus, time and place. The sounds of the kitchen, cans and bottles opening, crinkling bags, the smell of food in preparation, etc., will excite the chow hound, and soon the paws are in the air!

Here is the solution to stopping this behavior: Never give in to a beggar! You are rewarding the dog for sitting pretty, jumping up, whining and rubbing his nose into you by giving him that glorious reward—*food*. By ignoring the dog, you will (eventually) force the behavior into extinction. Note that the behavior likely gets worse before it disappears, so be sure there are not any "softies" in the family who will give in to little "Oliver" every time he whimpers, "More, please."

SEPARATION ANXIETY

Recognized by behaviorists as the most common form of stress for dogs, separation anxiety can also lead to your dog's resorting to destructive behaviors in your absence. It's more than your Foxhound's howling his displeasure at your leaving the house and his being left alone. This is a normal reaction, no different than the child who cries as his mother leaves him on the first day at school. Separation anxiety is more serious. In fact, if you are constantly with your dog, he will

Food stealing should not be tolerated. Not only is it improper behavior, it could cause the dog to become ill if he eats "people food" that's not good for him.

come to expect you with him all of the time, making it even more traumatic for him when you are not there.

Obviously, you enjoy spending time with your dog, and he thrives on your love and attention. However, it should not become a dependent relationship in which he is heartbroken without you. This broken heart can also bring on destructive behavior as well as loss of appetite, depression and lack of interest in play and interaction. Canine behaviorists have been spending much time and energy to help owners better understand the significance of this stressful condition.

One thing you can do to minimize separation anxiety is to make your entrances and exits as low-key as possible. Do not give your dog a long drawn-out goodbye, and do not lavish him with hugs and kisses when you return. This is giving in to the attention that he craves, and it will only make him miss it more when you are away. Another thing you can try is to give your dog a treat when you leave; this will not only keep him occupied and keep his mind off the fact that you have just left, but it will also help him associate your leaving with a pleasant experience.

You may have to accustom your dog to being left alone in intervals. Of course, when your

Anything within your Foxhound's reach is subject to inspection, so you must ensure that your "nosy" Foxhound doesn't snoop his way into danger.

dog starts whimpering as you approach the door, your first instinct will be to run to him and comfort him, but do not do it! Eventually he will adjust to your absence. His anxiety stems from being placed in an unfamiliar situation; by familiarizing him with being alone, he will learn that he will survive. That is not to say you should purposely leave your dog home alone, but the dog needs to know that, while he can depend on you for his care, you do not have to be by his side 24 hours a day. Some behaviorists recommend tiring the dog out before you leave home—take him for a good long walk or engage him in a game of fetch in the yard.

When the dog is alone in the house, he should be placed in his crate—another distinct advantage to crate-training your dog. The crate should be placed in his happy family area, where he normally sleeps and already feels comfortable, thereby making him feel more at ease when he is alone. Be sure to give the dog a special chew toy to enjoy while he settles into his crate.

INDEX

My English Foxhound

PUT YOUR PUPPY'S FIRST PICTURE HERE

Dog's Name _____

Date _____ Photographer _____